Our Teenage Years

Growing Up in a Small Town in the '80s

T.J.Wray

ISBN = 978-0-578-55338-2 (Paperback)

ISBN = 978-0-578-55339-9 (Digital)

Copyright © 2019 T. J. Wray

All rights reserved - First Edition

All rights reserved. No part of this publication may be reproduced, distributed, or transmitted in any form or by any means, including photocopying, recording, or other electronic or mechanical methods without the publisher's prior written permission. T. J. Wray

Contents

Introduction

In the Beginning

Mrs. ScottTerry

The Alligator Story

Margaret and My Truck

My Motorcycle Wreck

Just My Life

Growing up in a Small Town

The End of the Brown Beast!

Christy, Baby Melissa, and I

The Werewolf Story

A Different World

Just the way I'm Built

My House Burned Down!

Our Trip to Atlanta and the Georgia Dome

It's Just a Piece of Metal

Hodgepodge

Terry and My Dad

The End

Dedication

About the Author

Introduction

This story is about two best friends growing up in a small town in their teenage years. The trials and tribulations of going to school and dealing with their parents and siblings. As well as learning about girls, dealing with peer pressure, going to work and getting their first jobs. Plus, all the things we all did for the first time in our teenage years, like our first car and our first kiss. Also, all the fun stuff like chasing girls, shooting guns, riding motorcycles and three-wheelers, epic fishing trips, working on trucks, and just messing around with our friends.

This includes all the fights and troubles they got into at school or just trying to survive high school. As well as all the adventures and wild stories about exploring the backcountry roads and farmlands. Plus, all of their favorite fishing holes and hangout spots. It's an absolute miracle that they survived those teenage years! -- So, here is the story of my best friend Terry and me. Sadly Terry recently passed away.

This book is based on facts and is a true story to the very best of my memory. I put a lot of time, energy, and love into writing it. It brought up a lot of old stories and memories, some made me laugh, while others made me cry, I can only hope it does the same for you. Please enjoy reading it and share it with your loved ones.

I would like to apologize upfront if I offend anyone here because of my lack of command of the English language. I'm not politically correct and I don't speak proper English, I'm from Texas and I say Howdy, Y'all, and Ain't. I was always one of those students who preferred math and history, I still do, so please forgive me. Being from Texas makes English my second language, as Texan would be my first.

Chapter One

In the Beginning

Howdy, my name is T.J. I was born in 1968 in Texas. Things sure were different in 1968 than they are today. I think the population explosion has created all the new laws and rules we have to live by today, also, taxes are much higher today. Sometimes I wish I had been born in 1868 when things seemed much simpler. In those days if you had a problem with someone you went outside and settled it like men.

Anyway, in 1968 we lived in Burkburnett Texas where my dad and granddad worked in the booming oil fields of west Texas. Across the street from our little rented house lived my dad's mortal enemy (Sam), he was five or six years older than my dad. According to dad, he never liked this guy but he was always hanging around.

When I was two years old, my dad was twenty-six and my mom was twenty, I had a sister Katie who was two years older than me. So, in 1970 when I was two and Katie was four, my parents got divorced. After being together for six years and being married for four years, they were finished. Dad said that he used to come home from work and Sam would be sitting at his kitchen table. He hung around a lot and spent a lot of time with my mom while dad was at work.

They fought and fought about it, but dad said for months that he would come home and Sam would be in his house. So, after many, many fights they decided to get divorced. After working out the details they agreed that dad would take me and leave my sister with my mom.

Late one night after supper and another huge fight, (probably about Sam). He put me in the car and left, drove around the block and parked, sat there, and thought for a few minutes. Then leaving me in the car (at the age of two). He ran up the yard behind our house, jumped over the fence, and went through the back door to the house, grabbed my sister Katie and ran back out. Then he jumped in the car and took off. He later said to me, "I didn't want Sam the idiot raising my kids!"

We spent the next eleven years on the run! My sister and I recently sat down and figured it up. The closest we can remember (with input from friends and family), we lived in sixty-two different towns and seven different states during those eleven years of my life, between the ages of two and thirteen. We were really poor and always moving around.

Dad tried hard, most of the time working two jobs. The problem was that every time mom got close to finding us, or dad heard anything funny through the grapevine, or if someone came to his job asking around about us. Or just when anything happened, we would up and move away.

We left houses full of furniture, toys and clothes,

and everything we owned. If dad heard something funny that day he would just put us in the car and leave. He wouldn't go back to the house he would just drive all night and start all over in a new town, or a new state. We were always on the run and he couldn't keep a job so we were very, very poor.

We usually lived in places where we could stay for free like abandoned houses with no running water or electricity, sometimes not even any windows or doors. A lot of the time we lived on a farm or dairy where he could work and we could live there for free. I still remember him getting up at four a.m. to milk the cows. But a lot of the time we just lived in the car or in a roadside park (which is a rest area to most of you guys), we used to sleep on the picnic tables.

As I look back, I feel sorry for my dad, he had a good-paying job working in the oil fields of west Texas. Then he was forced to leave and spend eleven years on the run trying to raise me and my sister. I know he did the best he could though. It's funny because nowadays I'm a single dad trying to raise my two kids and it's majorly tough stuff.

When I was about four years old my dad met Brenda, my stepmom, they got married and she treated me and Katie like stepchildren for sure! She spanked us every day until we got big enough for beatings. My dad was a great big guy always around 350 lbs. or so, his waist size was like forty-six.

Brenda would take his belt and hold it by the buckle, like a whip. Then she would make me or my sister lie down on the bed and whip us with it. As we got older the beatings got more and more often, trying to keep us in line, I guess. I don't know for sure but sometimes I think she beat us daily just because she liked it, or she got some kind of kick out of it.

Brenda used to make me go cut a switch from a tree, every time she would say, "That's not big enough, Go cut another one!" I remember I would already be bawling my eyes out just cutting down a switch from a tree because I knew the beating was coming. She would make me pull down my pants, then she would beat and switch my bottom and legs until I had huge welts and was bleeding everywhere.

Many times, dad would come home from work and see me bleeding and crying. They would get into a huge fight and he would put Katie and me in his truck and leave. We would sleep in rest areas for two or three days, then they would make up and he would always go back to her. I don't think he knew how bad she beat us because usually when she was beating us, he was at work. They broke up many times over the years, but he always went back to her. When my dad died in 2010, he had been with Brenda for over thirty-five years.

In 1981 when I was thirteen and Katie was fifteen years old, after many years of Brenda beating us. I guess Katie had all she could take, she ran away from home with our next-door neighbor who was like thirty years old. Katie, who was four years old when my parents got divorced, had memories of our mother. I was only two when they got divorced, and at thirteen years old I had no memories of my mother. Katie ran away with the neighbor guy to go find our mother.

At the time (1981), we lived in Corpus Christi, Texas. We didn't know it yet but mom lived in Guthrie, Oklahoma, thirty-five miles north of Oklahoma City, with Sam the idiot and their two kids. It took Katie about two months, with help from friends and relatives, to find our mother.

When Katie found mom, she told her where I was at and soon mom started writing me letters. Dad was reluctant at first to even let me read them, but eventually, he did. Then after a while he even decided, (if she would buy the plane ticket), I could go to Guthrie, Oklahoma for a visit and meet her.

As I said, I had no memory of her and I had never been on an airplane before, to say the least, I was scared to death! So, during Christmas break in the seventh grade in 1981, I got on a plane and flew to

Oklahoma City, to meet my mother for the first time, at the age of thirteen. As I remember it was nice meeting mom and she seemed nice, but dad was right, Sam was an idiot! He hated me from the very first day.

He hated me because I looked like my dad and I had my dad's last name. Everything about me reminded Sam the idiot of my dad. I lived with Sam and my mom for four and a half years and he only hit me once. But he was always mean to me and favored his other kids over me in every way, and he liked to prove it to me.

Especially around the holidays. Sam wouldn't let mom buy me things for Christmas or my birthday. She was only allowed to buy me one present, while the other kids got lots of presents. I guess because she didn't work and the money was his money, he didn't want her to spend his money on me. Finally, just after my eighteenth birthday, I got into a huge fight with Sam the idiot. I moved out of his house and never looked back.

Chapter Two

Mrs. Scott

In 1981 when I was thirteen and a half years old, I moved to Guthrie Oklahoma. Initially, I was supposed to just visit and meet my mother and her family, I was supposed to go back home in three days. I came in the middle of the school year during Christmas break when I was in seventh grade. Mom, however, tricked me into staying, now that I look back. In the week before my arrival, she learned that the paper route, (right in her neighborhood) was available, the old paperboy had quit for some reason.

She knew in the back of her mind how extremely poor I had been growing up and she used that against me. She told me I could get the job and make a lot of money. I said, "Yeah right! Like how much money?" She said, "Probably like $200 a month." I remember going upstairs to the room I shared with my half-brother and I thought for a long time. I was thinking that the downside would be staying in Sam's house, but the upside was $200 a month. 'Damn, I would be rich!' I do not think I had ever owned more than .50 cents at one time before that, $200 sounded like a million bucks to me.

Even though Sam the idiot hated me and I hated being at his house, it was still better than living with Brenda and taking those beatings every day. Brenda's abuse was physical, Sam's abuse was verbal and mental. At least when he was finished cursing and screaming at me, I could go to my room and ignore him.

I am sure there are a lot of kids out there that are in the same boat I was in as a teenager. If I had it to do over, I would go and talk to a counselor at school or my church, about all the fighting that went on between my mom and stepdad. And about how he treated me and yelled and cursed me daily, or how uncomfortable it was living in his house. I now know that when you are a teenager, you are old enough to say something. You should not have to live in an abusive environment. So, my advice would be to seek help in these types of situations.

I see more and more teenagers on the news these days. Who ended up doing something really, really bad to either themselves or someone else. So again, my advice is to seek help from a counselor or even a teacher at school. There must be a teacher at your school, or a person at church, maybe even a neighbor, that you like and can go talk to in private. Just do not wait and let it go so far that you end up doing something you will regret, then you end up paying for it, for the rest of your life.

I still remember the phone call I had to make to my dad to tell him I was not coming home, I was in tears as I tried my best to explain. 'I did not like Sam,' but I was staying because I had applied to the paper office and gotten the job. I told him that I was going to be working and making money as well as going to school. He was very upset and disappointed with me, you could hear it in his voice.

After that day I didn't speak to my dad for almost three years, when I finally did talk to him, he was in Wisconsin. He told me after Katie and I left, he contemplated committing suicide, but then decided to move to Canada. He got as far as Wisconsin and ran out of money, where he learned that there is still free government land in upstate Wisconsin. All you have to do is move onto it, build a house and take care of it, and pay the property taxes each year and it is your land. My dad lived the remaining thirty years of his life in Wisconsin with Brenda, where he passed away in 2010.

I got the paper route, my first job, I had 130 customers. The newspapers came six days a week in a large bundle dropped off in my mom's front yard. When I got home from school each day the papers were sitting right there just waiting for me to deliver them to my customers.

I had to roll each one individually with a rubber band. Then on wet or snowy days, I had to put each paper into a plastic sleeve. It took about thirty minutes for me to roll the papers and put them in my delivery bags. I carried two large delivery bags draped across my shoulders hanging off of each side of my bicycle, I could run my route in about an hour on a nice day.

I took pride in my work and gave my home phone number to all of my customers. If someone didn't get their paper (I know I delivered it), but if a dog ate it, or someone stole it, all they had to do was call me, I would run another one over to them. I took good care of my customers because I didn't want to lose any of them. *It would make me look bad at the paper office I thought.* So, no matter the weather condition, for two years, I always got the job done!

I still remember my first paycheck, I collected from

all of my customers and paid my paper bill at the paper office. Then whatever was left was my pay for the month. I got $128 for the first month, I was rich! I had never seen $128 before. I did the math, the paper came six days a week (no paper on Saturday), and I had 130 customers. That meant I had to deliver a little over three thousand papers each month to get that $128.

I worked hard, I did not want to lose a single one of those 130 customers, who represented about a dollar each in my pocket each month. Plus, all the little old ladies who loved me were always baking me cookies and bread and all kinds of sweets. At the ripe old age of thirteen and a half, I was a proud member of the American workforce.

At the very end of my paper route, there was a nursing home, just about three miles west of mom's house. I had about fifteen customers inside this nursing home. The old paperboy used to just leave the fifteen papers at the front desk and let the nurses give them to the patients. I wanted to meet and get to know all of my customers, so I took each paper to the room it belonged to and met the customer personally. Those old people were some of the nicest people I have ever met. They always had a big smile and were happy to see me. When I came out of the far end of the nursing home, I was done for the day with my paper route.

Right across the street from the nursing home was a small mom-and-pop hamburger stand. It was a little white brick building with a drive-up window and one picnic table beside the building, with a gravel driveway. You couldn't go inside, just a drive-up window to order from. You had to get your food and take it home or eat at that one old picnic table. Most people just took the food home or ate in their car. Every day after I finished my paper route and came out of that nursing home, I would go across the street to Mr. Chappell's hamburger stand.

Mr. Chappell really liked me, and he would give me a big brown paper sack full of French fries every day, and I would give him a free newspaper. He always told me the fries were just leftovers from the day and not to worry about paying for them. I think he knew what time I would be coming each day and he made the fries fresh just before I got there. Funny, right? They were really good homemade fries, they weren't in a container but just dumped into a brown paper bag. I would sit down at that old picnic table, tear open the bag, put some ketchup on the side and enjoy! I did this just about every day for two years during my paper route. Mr. Chappell really liked me, even years later when he'd see me around town, he would always stop and shake my hand and say, "Hello."

Anyway, I started carving a poem into that old picnic table with my pocket knife. It took me a couple of months to write this poem because I didn't know what to say or how to word it, I had never written anything before. So, I would carve a word or two in the picnic table and then wait a few days and think about what I wanted to say, then I would carve another word or two. After about a month and a half, I finally had it and I was proud of it! It read-

>I was here but now I'm gone
>
>I left my name to turn you on
>
>I'll be back before you know it
>
>This don't rhyme cause I'm no poet
>
>T. J.

A couple of months ago I picked my ten-year-old daughter up from school one day. She was just about in tears and said, "The teacher is making us all write a poem and I do not know how to write a poem. I have been trying all day and I can't do it! I tried to write about my dog but nothing rhymes with his name, (Link). I tried to write about my dolls or toys but I cannot do it, I don't know how to write it!"

I said, "Well, I have only written one poem in my life and you are welcome to use it. You probably will not get into trouble for plagiarizing your own father." So that night she wrote it out just as I told her.

> I was here but now I'm gone
>
> I left my name to turn you on
>
> I'll be back before you know it
>
> This don't rhyme cause I'm no poet
>
> Rose

She turned it in to her teacher the next morning. She got a (B) on it, we laughed and laughed. Can you believe she got a B on that poem some thirty-five years later after I chiseled it into that old picnic table? How funny.

I always try to be a better parent than my parents were. I try to be there for my kids and give them all the things I did not have when I was a kid and help them in any way I can. I hope you do the same!

Guthrie Junior High School

Going back to school after that Christmas break in 1981 wasn't so easy. I was in a strange land, at a new school, and knew no one, I was lost and scared to death! I still remember my first day at Guthrie Junior High School. All the other kids had been going to that school for months and knew exactly where to go. I came in the middle of the school year and I was lost, to say the least.

Guthrie Junior High School is a 3-story building with a thousand classrooms. I had never seen a school that had more than one floor before. In grade school, you always went to one classroom all day and had one teacher. In junior high, you went to a different classroom every hour and had a different teacher for each class. This freaking school was huge, I was lost and scared to death! I did not know anybody, I did not know where to go. I did not know which book went with which class, and I was afraid to ask anyone. I could not even get my locker open, I did not know how to work the combination. Again, I was scared absolutely and completely to death!

I was late for my first four classes because I could not find them. If you got to the class after the bell rang you were "tardy," and you got a tardy slip. I did not know it yet but if you got more than three tardy slips in a single month, you got detention! Hell, I got five tardy slips on my first day! I did not even know what detention was, but I would soon find out.

Detention meant that you got to stay an hour after school, sit in a very quiet room and do your homework or read a book. The problem was, if you stayed for an hour after school you would miss the bus. I had to call my mom to pick me up an hour after school on my very first day, you talk about humiliating.

That story reminds me of another story. As I said,

I was late for my first four classes, then I went to lunch. I was not about to be late for my fifth class. So, while I was on lunch break I went looking for my fifth-hour class.

By the way, I had gotten on an airplane for the first time in my life two weeks earlier and flew from Corpus Christi Texas to Oklahoma City. I was scared to death and shaking in my boots, I got on the plane and looked for my seat number. The lady in the seat next to me was a beautiful sandy blond with a terrific smile. She was very sweet, with a calming soft voice, and she reminded me of Brooke Shields.

I asked if I could sit by the window and look out and she said, "Sure" and she traded seats with me. She said, "Hi, my name is Cindy", I said, "Hi, I'm T. J." The plane ride was like two and a half hours and the whole way Cindy kept me calm. I told her that I had never been on an airplane before, we talked about everything.

She asked what I had gotten for Christmas, where

I was from, and about my parents, we just talked and talked. I think she was trying to take my mind off of the flight and keep me calm. Anyway, she was so sweet and one of the nicest people I have ever met. At the Oklahoma City terminal, I thanked her for everything and said goodbye.

Now let us go back to that fifth-hour class.

On my lunch break, I found a teacher outside and I asked him where the music room was. At Guthrie Junior High School, you had to go outside the main building, about thirty yards, to get to the shop class. We had a woodshop and a metal shop, and right above the shop classes was the music room.

I was not going to be late again, so, I went straight to the music classroom instead of going to the cafeteria for lunch. I got there about fifteen minutes early so no one was in there, and I sat in the back of the class and waited.

The kids started coming in and in a few minutes, the teacher came in. She walked right up to the chalkboard and started writing something with her back to us. She said, "All right now take your seats and be quiet." Then, just as the classroom went quiet, she turned around to face us. All of a sudden, just as she turned around, I blurted out in a way too loud voice, "Cindy!" Everyone in there just busted out laughing, It took her about five minutes to calm the students down.

Then she said, "T.J. you must be our new student?" I said, "Yes, ma'am." She said, "I am Mrs. Scott your music teacher and I will talk with you after class." Gosh, was I ever embarrassed, but I was happy to finally find someone I knew at this new school. Mrs. Scott was my favorite teacher at Guthrie Junior High School, I really enjoyed her class. We sang in the choir and learned how to play flutes and ukulele. I did not know Terry yet, but he was in that music class also. We both took her class as an elective the following year together.

Chapter Three

Terry

As I said, I really enjoyed Mrs. Scott's music class. It was easy to find my sixth-hour class, it was right downstairs from the music room, a shop class. During the first semester, they had a woodshop class. However, since I came after Christmas and it was the second semester we had a metal-shop class.

On the third day of going to this new school, I got swats, from our metal shop teacher Mr. Prince, for something (I did not do!). This means I got paddled with a big board. In the 1980s teachers gave students paddlings or swats when they got in trouble, but to my memory, it was only the male teachers who gave swats. The shop teachers and coaches all did, and our principal was always a big black man and he liked giving swats. If you got swats from him there was a good chance you would never do whatever you got in trouble for again.

Anyway, on the third day of school in shop class, we had these giant architecture-type desks in the metal shop. The kid behind me (Randle McGee), was eating sunflower seeds and throwing the shells under my desk. When Mr. Prince saw the shells he threw a fit! I told him it was not me, but he just said, "Go out into the hallway and wait for me," in a very stern voice. A few minutes later he came out with his giant wooden paddle that I had seen hanging above his desk, he gave me five swats. I did not cry because I did not want to give McGee the satisfaction, but man did those swats hurt!

So, after school on the third day, I confronted that kid, Randle McGee, who had been throwing shells under my desk, and we started yelling and pushing each other. I did not realize it but he had an older brother who also went to our school. Pretty soon his brother Lee was also pushing me and yelling at me.

Terry, who was in that shop class and knew exactly what that kid had done was walking by on his way out of the school. Terry stopped and yelled something at one of the McGee brothers, and wouldn't you know it, as soon as they realized it was going to be two against two instead of two against one, they backed down.

It is fair to say that Terry and I became best buddies from that moment onwards, and he always had my back and I had his. We looked alike, both short and fat, and we were always together, so everybody thought we were brothers. Even years later someone would see me at Walmart or somewhere and ask, "Where is your brother?", and I knew exactly who they were talking about.

Shocking!

As I said, Terry and I were best friends and were

always together. We picked the same electives so we would have classes together. In the eighth grade, we picked music and shop class just like the year before. In the eighth-grade shop class, we really got that kid back for the seeds he had spit under my desk, and the swats I ended up getting.

In the metal shop, we had an ancient-looking kind of medieval, spot-welding machine. It had these two giant arms that were spring-loaded. You press down on a big pedal, and they come together in the middle. You put your piece of metal that you wanted to weld in between the two arms. Then, with a huge electrical spark flying, metal-melting shock wave, it would spot-weld your two pieces of metal together.

So, one day it was Terry and my day to sweep up. We knew that this McGee kid, who we didn't like, was going to use the spot-welder next. So, we "accidentally" moved the rubber mat you were supposed to stand on at the spot welder. Terry and I were standing over in the corner watching as this kid stepped up on the platform and placed his piece in the welder and then stepped down on the big pedal to turn the welder on.

Sparks went flying from the welder, and the kid screamed as he got the crap shocked out of him. He went flying about ten feet and landed on his butt, everybody in the room started laughing. Mr. Prince ran out from his office and yelled, "How many times do I have to tell y'all, you cannot use the spot-welder unless the rubber mat is in place, you will be shocked!" Man, we laughed about that for weeks, every time we saw that kid we would just crack up.

I am not sure how many fights we got into over the years with the McGee brothers, but I do not think anyone ever really won! I do remember the last big fight though. Everybody in school had been talking about it for weeks, and probably a hundred people showed up to watch. We were going to fight the McGee boys one last time and shut them up for good. The fight was to take place about dusk at Mineral Wells Park. There was only one rule, (No Weapons), you had to fight with what you were born with.

Terry and I showed up with about four or five of our friends and the McGee brothers showed up with about four or five of their friends. We walked towards each other and the fight was on, nobody said anything, we just kind of attack each other! It was an all-out brawl, a melee for about twenty minutes. Then the cops showed up and we scattered like flies. That was the last time I saw the McGee brothers, I guess they moved away after that summer. Another tough life lesson learned for me though, (ouch!) As I said, it is a miracle we survived those teenage years. Some of our earlier fights included knives, hammers, and even saw blades. We learned early that it is much fairer and much less painful to just fight with what you were born with.

I will give you another example of Terry having my

back. A few years later I called over to his house and his mom answered the phone. I said, "Is Terry there?" She replied, "No, I sent him to the store to get me some cigarettes, he will be back in a few minutes." I said, "Okay, can you have him call me or come over? I have got some trouble and need his help." She said, "Sure, I will." About fifteen minutes later he came flying down the road.

My mother's house was the last house on a dead-end dirt road. He came tearing down the road, parked and ran into the house. Without even knocking he slings open the front door and starts yelling, "T. J.! T. J.! Where are you at? Are you okay?" I peeked around, from the kitchen and said, "What the hell are you doing man?" You should have seen the serious look on his face. Terry owned an old .38 pistol that had belonged to his grandfather, and it was sticking out of the front of his pants. He said, "Mom said you were in trouble and needed my help." The look on his face would have cut right through you. I said, "Man I am fine, my truck won't start and I am late for work, I need a ride."

We laughed about it afterward, but that goes to show you that any time there was any trouble, or Terry thought there was trouble, he always had my back. Thanks, buddy.

Patricia

When we were teenagers Terry was really big into square dancing. He went all the time and was always inviting me and asking me to go with him. But I was like, "I do not dance man, and in a square, what is that all about?" He just kept asking though. Then he started talking about this girl he met at square dancing and really wanted me to meet her.

I finally gave in and went one night, it was late one evening inside one of the grade school gymnasiums. We went up to the door and he pointed her out across the gym. There were a lot of people there and I was like, "Where? Which one?" He said, "Right over there, the one in the blue dress, her name is Patricia!"

I am here to tell you guys that this girl was like nine years old, skinny as a rail, and nothing but knees and elbows. I laughed and said, "Whatever man! Where is her big sister?" He looked at me as serious as he could possibly look and said, "I am serious, I am going to wait for her to grow up a little bit and I am going to ask her parents if I can take her out." We were fourteen and fifteen at the time.

I was a year older than everybody else in my grade because I had failed the second grade and had to take it twice. The first year I was in the second grade, I went to seven different schools because we moved around so much, and I flunked and had to do the second grade again. Anyway, Terry was madly in love with Patricia and he knew very early that he wanted to spend the rest of his life with her. I do not think he was scared to ask her out, but he was terrified of talking to her parents about it! So, he waited.

A few months later I went by Terry's house one day after school and his mom had just gotten him a brand-new computer and a printer. By the way, Terry taught himself how to type on that computer, he could type sixty words a minute, self-taught, I was amazed. Anyway, he figured out how to use the printer, and the first thing he did was make a giant banner that went all the way around his room. It said 'Terry Loves Patricia', in huge letters. You could see this thing from the road in front of their house, Terry's room faced the street. Well, you knew it was serious then because he put it up on the wall for the whole world to see. This was the only time in my life that I experienced love at first sight.

Terry loved that girl from the first moment he met her, and he did not want to be with any other girls. I think this kept him out of trouble, especially in those early years. Patricia was always in the back of his mind and he was waiting for her to grow up a little. I know in high school I liked chasing girls, I liked looking at girls and wanted to be with them. I used to carry a big book in front of me when I walked down the hall. This book was not for studying, it was because I was looking at the girls and did not want to be embarrassed:).

Terry never had these problems because Patricia was in the back of his mind and that kept him away from the parties and on the straight and narrow. So, whether she knew or not, she had a big influence on him, especially in those early years. Terry and Patricia were married for over twenty years until he passed away in 2016. Thank you, Patty, for being there for him all those years. I know it was not always easy on you and the girls, but I am glad you were there with him.

Fake IDs

Terry and I had fake IDs when we were seventeen and eighteen that said we were twenty-one. We got them from a girl who worked at the tag office who went to our school, her mother ran the tag office. We got into a lot of trouble over the years with those IDs. We were afraid to use them in Guthrie because in a small town everybody knows you. So, we would go to Oklahoma City and try to get into clubs. A couple of times we actually got in and even bought drinks at the bar, but most of the time they just ran us out at the door.

One night we were trying to get into this new country and western club in Oklahoma City, they almost called the cops. Terry talked them into calling his mother instead. By the time she drove the thirty-five miles to Oklahoma City, she was so mad that her hair was practically on fire! The security guard released us into her custody after she promised to never allow us to come back to his club. She chewed our butts out for weeks over that, and she cut up our fake IDs. We never did that again! Lesson learned.

Chapter Four

The Alligator Story

One of our favorite things to do during our teenage years was going fishing, we had a lot of favorite fishing holes. Guthrie has two main lakes, Lake Guthrie, where there are too many houses around and usually too many people around. And Liberty Lake, which is more secluded and has bigger and better fish. But really for our money, the best fishing holes were found off the beaten path or on "Private Property," as some people call it.

We used to just drive around in my truck in the warm evenings, or on weekends looking for a nice farm pond or really anything we could fish in. If we saw something we liked, we did not ask permission. We just jumped over the fence and went fishing until someone said otherwise.

Anyway, one day while we were out cruising the back-country roads looking for a new fishing hole when we came upon a promising-looking place. It was a nicely sized farm pond with some trees on one side, to hide us from view. The cows were way down at the other end of the property. So, we jumped over the fence and started fishing. We had just been there for a few minutes when we both, about the same time, noticed a dead tree on the other side of the pond that kept moving back and forth in the water.

Terry looked at me and said, "What the hell is that?" I said, "I don't know, but let's check it out." So, as we walked along the bank. I was going slow, still trying to fish as I walked, but we kept seeing this tree moving in the water, so we hurried over to it. There was something in the water next to the tree, but we could not get a good look at it because of the murky water. It looked like an old car tire or something black and rubbery looking. Curious as we were, we started throwing rocks at it, but it did not move. So, we started poking it with the ends of our fishing poles, trying to figure out what it was.

Then all of a sudden a giant alligator reared up out of the water and lunged directly towards us! Turned out the tire-looking thing was the end of its tail. We both screamed like little girls and fell backward and dropped our fishing poles. You did not know fat boys could run that fast! We lost all of our fishing equipment that day. We were too scared to go back and get it. I remember as we were running for our lives, Terry looked at me and said, "Well, if we survive this we will have a hell of a story to tell our grandkids". Nobody had to tell us that it was private property, we never went back in there again!

We had lots of favorite fishing holes, like 'The Tree.' This was a place across the street from Guthrie Lake, kind of a runoff from the lake. There is a giant old oak tree deep in the trees, real private, right next to the water. We used to swing off of a long piece of rope tied to that giant old oak tree into the water. This was a favorite spot for a lot of our friends in high school. We would go out there and watch the sunset and the stars come out. I am sure a lot of us lost our virginity, during our teenage years, at this very spot.

Another place we liked to fish, or just shoot our guns, was a place we called 'The Mouth.' There are two main rivers in Guthrie, the Cottonwood River that runs right through the middle of town and floods half the town every spring, and the Cimarron River that runs just on the outer edge of town. Just north of the high school, off an old dirt road in a secluded spot these two rivers run together in a spot we called 'The Mouth.'

We would (snag-fish), at the mouth. I believe snag fishing is illegal, but it works great! You just tie some giant three-way hooks on your line and cast it out and snag the fish, you do not need any bait! We would catch giant catfish and even bigger giant Alligator Gar! A Gar has a long snout, kind of like a spoonbill fish with lots and lots of teeth.

We would catch these giant six-foot Gar. We would stab their snout into the sand and watch them flop around. Some people eat Gar, but I have been told that they are very bony and not very good for eating, we never ate one. However, we did eat catfish, bass, crappie, perch, or anything else we could catch.

There was a big railroad trestle that went across the Mouth and we would set up on it and shoot our guns. You can shoot the gar as they break the surface of the water to take a breath. It really sucked when you got caught on that railroad bridge when a train was coming through. You could stand off to the side and hold on to one of the support beams (and not die!), but man, was it loud as the train went by, and you would think that you were going to die. Yeah, we liked to go fishing or go ride my three-wheeler or dirt bike or shoot our guns. With my paper route, I saved up and got lots of cool stuff.

Role Model

I challenge you guys right now! If you are a man, lead by example, be a positive role model. You can not tell your kids not to smoke if you smoke two packs a day because they are going to want to grow up and be just like you. I do not care if it is drugs or alcohol or cigarettes or just bad parenting, Stop! and be a positive role model, Lead by example! These kids nowadays do not have enough role models. Do you really want your kid's role models to be Kanye East, Miley Vyrus, and the Bieb? Give me a break!

If you do not have kids or grandkids or neighbor kids, go volunteer at a youth group or youth camp or Boy Scouts or Royal Rangers or YMCA. Go take a kid to play basketball or take a kid four-wheeling or dirt biking or teach a kid how to fish or shoot pool. This will be very fulfilling in your life and will change the kid's life. It might even save a kid's life from a life of drugs or gang violence. Be a role model, I challenge you, do not wait, do it today! Take a poor kid like I was and teach him to fish or ride a motorcycle or four-wheeler, it is life-changing!

I still remember the positive role models in my impressionable teenage years, and I think about them often. People like Randy and Mike who I had worked for taught me the value of a dollar and the value of an honest hard day's work. These guys were real men, they did not smoke or drink or do drugs. The leaders in my Royal Ranger troop taught me how to camp and fish and how to shoot black powder, and our youth pastor and all the good that he did leading our youth group. These were real men, and I still try to imitate them in my life today. I challenge you guys to be a positive role model to a kid today! I recently went back to school to get my teaching degree in Education that I started almost thirty years ago. I truly believe we need more good teachers and positive role models for our teenagers today, probably more so than ever before.

Chapter Five

Margaret and My Truck

Margaret

I met Margaret during my freshman year in high school, we were the same age, but she was a grade ahead of me in school. As I said, I failed the second grade and was held back a year. She was my first girlfriend, we hit it off and started dating and I thought she was beautiful. We were the perfect couple and people called us "Samson and Delilah." I was big and strong, always working out, she was about ninety pounds soaking wet. We dated for three years in high school and I took her to her junior and senior prom.

After dating for about a year I gave her a promise ring, and she wore it on a gold chain around her neck. Margaret was my high school sweetheart, I loved her dearly and would have died for her. We spent a lot of time together and did everything together from helping each other with homework to spending time at the 'Tree' watching the stars. We hung out a lot at the bowling alley, it was the only place in town that had video games and pool tables, our friends were always there.

Guthrie had an old-fashioned drive-in movie theater, and on Tuesday nights, they had carload night. You could get into the movies with as many people as you can fit in your car, all for the price of one regular person on any other night. So, we would put like fifteen people in the back of my truck and go to the drive-in on Tuesday nights. Margaret and I spent a lot of time at the drive-in, it was one of our favorite things to do. She was a single child and lived with her mother and stepfather, her stepdad was a strict, mean old man. The more I could keep her out of the house, the happier she was.

The first year we went to the prom, I was so nervous. I had never had a monkey suit on before and I had never danced with a girl before. She looked awesome though, before the prom, I took her to the fanciest restaurant in Guthrie. It was a black-tie-only place that was on the upper floor of one of the old buildings downtown. We had swordfish and the meal cost fifty dollars, the most expensive meal I had ever eaten, by far.

The next year we went to the prom again and she was beautiful in her prom dress. She wore a blue dress and I wore a matching blue tuxedo. We danced and had a great time at the prom. All of our friends were there and I was not so nervous now that I had done this before. When we left, we drove around behind the high school and made out for an hour in my truck. I remember that I had her dress halfway over her head. I was having a good old time when all of a sudden, I saw a giant spotlight in my face! It was a Guthrie cop, and he asked to see our IDs. Her birthday was two months ahead of mine. When he saw our IDs, she was eighteen and I was seventeen. He just told me to take her home and not to be back behind the school after hours anymore. I often wondered what he would have done if it were the other way around and she had been seventeen and I was eighteen.

Margaret graduated the year before I did and it screwed everything up. After graduation, she got a job at McDonald's and everything changed. During that summer I used to go out there and see her every day, she would give me free French fries. The problem was that I had to go back to school in the fall, and she wanted to move to the city and start college, I was screwed. I loved her dearly, and I thought we would get married and have kids one day. She wore my promise ring around her neck, but none of that mattered now, I had lost her to the world. She met some guy that came through the drive-through at McDonald's, and she was gone. There was nothing I could do about it.

The last time I saw her she stopped by the furniture store where I worked and gave me my ring back. I was crushed and furious at the same time. I threw the ring at the rolled-down window on my truck when she gave it to me. I spent four hours after work that day looking for that ring. I was hoping I could find it and give it back to her someday, but I never found it. I sat in the McDonald's parking lot, every day after work for three weeks hoping she would show up, but she never did. Just like that, she was gone! I was heartbroken, but life goes on.

My First Truck

During the first year, I had a paper route, I saved every penny I made. When I was fourteen, I bought my first motorcycle. Then at fourteen and a half, I got my motorcycle driving license. I had freedom as I had never known before! I took myself to school and anywhere else I wanted to go. In the eighth grade, I was driving myself to school while all the other kids still rode the bus or depended on their parents to take them everywhere. You cannot even imagine the freedom that I was now experiencing, I could go anywhere!

A few months later I used the rest of my savings to buy my first truck, it was a 1953 Chevy pickup. (Because of that truck, I am and shall always be a Chevy guy.) It looked like crap when I first got it, but I loved that truck. I had worked hard and saved hard for that truck and was very proud to own it. I had every bolt out of that truck at one time or another. Terry and I used to drive it to Stillwater Oklahoma, every day to go to Vo-Tech. One day coming back from Vo-Tech, I blew the engine and had to rebuild it.

Another time, the transmission went out and it took me three weeks to rebuild it. I did not have any help, and I had never done it before. Unlike kids today who just Google it or watch a YouTube video. I had to learn everything the hard way, by trial and error or the process of elimination. We had to actually go to the library and read books to learn things:) I did all the bodywork and painted it, I replaced all the suspension and shocks as well as the kingpins, which were almost impossible to get out. I even replaced the wood in the bed and stained and varnished it.

I put on white wagon wheels with small tires up front and giant mud tires on the back. Safe to say, I loved that truck. Terry and I wore that thing out driving the backroads and exploring the countryside. I drove it all the way through high school and several years thereafter. I even at one point sold it and bought it back two years later because I missed it and was afraid it was not being taken care of. Everybody in town knew my truck and when they saw it they knew I was coming, even the cops.

I bought the truck when I turned fifteen, I had six months to learn how to drive it before getting my (car) driving permit. I practiced every day after I finished my paper route. I taught myself how to drive that old stick shift truck in my mom's pasture, without help from anyone! When I was fifteen, I had never driven anything except my motorcycle and three-wheeler.

That truck was a four-speed with granny gear.

The problem was because it was so old, all the numbers were already worn off the shifter knob before I got it, I could not tell which gear was where. I did not know how to use a clutch, except on my bike, and it is on the handlebars. I could not figure out which gear to take off in or how to find the next gear. Another problem was the pasture was only so big and by circling it, I could only get up to about thirty before I had to shut it down because I ran out of room. So again, I learned by trial and error and the process of elimination.

After three excruciating, tumultuous months in the pasture every day after school, I finally learned enough to go down the alley and onto the dirt road behind mom's place. I was not very comfortable for a long time, but after a month or so of practice on the road, I felt good enough to go take my driving test. However, practicing out in the country there was not anywhere to parallel park. I took the driving test and failed it three times because I could not figure out how to parallel park that truck. Finally, on the fourth try, I got my driving permit.

The summer before I turned sixteen, I took driver's ed at the high school. I took it because I heard that it would help lower my insurance cost. After three weeks in the classroom with about thirty other students, who were all there to get their driving permit, and after three weeks of studying books and films about safe driving. On the last day of the class, as we were about to take the written exam to get our permits to drive, the instructor called each of us up to his desk. Each student had to show two forms of ID before taking the written test. All the other kids brought their birth certificates and social security cards. When he called me up, I flopped down my social security card and my driver's license! He said, "How did you get a driver's license before your sixteenth birthday?" I said, "It is a motorcycle license and I have had it for over a year! I have been driving myself around for over a year."

He said, "You do not have to take this test. It is the same written test you already took when you got your motorcycle license. All you have to do is go down to the DMV and show your license, take the driving test (pass it), and you will have your permit." It was pretty funny. All those other kids were there to get a driver's license and I already had mine for over a year. They all looked at me funny as I walked out and left them to take the exam.

Terry's Parents

One day I went over to Terry's house to help his dad pull a tree stump from their front yard with my truck, it had granny gear and you could pull the world with it. Terry's parents loved me, they treated me better than my own parents ever did.

Terry's mom was one of my favorite people during my teenage years, she loved me and treated me like one of her own. She used to tell me that she wished she had a daughter so I could marry into her family. She thought the world of me, and I really liked her. She even loaned me her car to drive for a year when I was in college. My truck broke down and she did not want me to stop going to college, so she loaned me her car to drive. Do you know anybody who is not related to you who would loan you a car for a year? Yeah, she really liked me.

She was an awesome cook, you could smell what she was cooking as you walked up to her driveway before you even got into the house. She cooked stews, chili, and homemade pies and bread, but my favorite was the beans and homemade cornbread. She made cornbread with an old cast-iron skillet, it was to die for. That was probably the reason why we boys were all so big!

And Terry's dad liked me too, I was always helping him work on something. I would come over and he would say, "Thank God, T. J. is here. I got these three lazy boys who will not do anything around here!" (Terry was a middle child; he had an older brother and a younger brother.) "Every time you come over," he said,

"You jump right in and help me." Then, he would say, "Hand me those pliers, we are working on the washing machine today."

He did not know it but I was just earning my keep, because I was planning on staying for supper! I used to joke that I spent more time, and ate more meals at Terry's house than I did at my mom's house. But it was true, I did! I really liked Terry's mom and dad, they helped me a lot in those teenage years, and I still miss them. It is funny how the people whom you do not realize are making an impact on you, leave such a lasting impression on your life. Rest in peace, my friends…

Chapter Six

My Motorcycle Wreck

A Real Job

After I had my paper route for two years, I was now fifteen and a half and ready for a real job. I had my truck, my motorcycle, and Margaret (my sweetheart), all I needed now was a real job. For the two years, I had lived with my mom she always babysat a little boy about five years old named Levi. Levi's father owned and operated the oldest and largest furniture store in Guthrie. With just one phone call from mom, I had an interview.

I made the very best out of that interview, I wore my Sunday best and presented myself well. I really, really wanted that job. I told Mike the owner, that not only did I have my motorcycle license for a year, with a perfect driving record, but also, I now had my driving permit to drive a car. As long as I had a licensed driver in the vehicle with me, I could drive the delivery truck and deliver furniture for him.

The timing could not have been better, Mike had just had an old guy retire, and he needed the help. The only help he had was another old guy that had one foot in the retirement chair too. It was perfect because the old guy could ride around with me and watch me do all the work. For the next three years, I did all the driving and ninety percent of the work. Mike paid me a salary of $175 a week, he paid me in cash every Friday, like contract labor, he did not take out taxes.

My God, I was rich! I had been making $130 a month with the paper route and only getting paid once a month. Getting a paycheck of $175 every Friday was like being a millionaire! I worked hard and made Mike proud to have me on his payroll. I worked every day after school and ten hours on Saturdays. I put in thirty or thirty-five hours each week, and I loved the job. I learned a lot on that job that is still with me today. We laid carpet and tile, did service calls on all kinds of appliances, and delivered and refinished all kinds of furniture. Thanks, Mike, there were a lot of great life lessons I learned on that job, and they stayed with me for the rest of my life!

In the summertime, I had two jobs, I worked at the furniture store for Mike, and I worked on the hay wagon for Randy, Randy was like a father figure to me. As I said, my dad did not speak to me for almost three years after I left. Randy was the greatest role model to me in those early impressionable teenage years. He was a hardworking, easy-going, laid-back kind of guy; and I never heard him cuss or lose his temper. If I had a problem in school or with girls or with my truck or anything. Randy always had time to talk to me about it, and he usually had the answer. I was lucky to have those two bosses in my life, and I really liked working for both of them. I do not know what happened to Mike, I lost track of him many years ago, but I still go by and see Randy from time to time. He is getting old, but he is still one of the good guys, they do not make 'em like that anymore.

My Motorcycle Wreck

In high school, I used to give Terry a ride home after school on the back of my motorcycle. He lived over on the west side of town, the high school was on the east side. One day as I was running him home really quickly, so I could get to work, it had just started to rain. We were going about 40 mph down a side street, just about a mile from his house.

Then suddenly, a lady pulled out in front of me. We slammed into the right front fender of her car, and we both went flying over her car! We bounced off of her windshield, busting it out, and landed in the middle of the street on the other side of her car. We did not wear helmets in those days.

I was lying in the middle of the street, and Terry

had bounced off of me and rolled over by the curb. He was just wailing and crying and screaming, he kept screaming, "Ouch! Ouch! Ouch!" He was gasping for air and choking at the same time, I thought he was dying. I remember lying in that street with tears in my eyes, thinking I had just killed my best friend. I broke my left ankle in the wreck and I could not stand up. I crawled over to him and said, "Hang in there man, they are on their way."

I could already hear the sirens coming down the block, by the time they got there, I was bawling. The ambulance guy came running up to me and I said, "I am fine, Go get him. He is dying!" They grabbed Terry, put him on a stretcher, and loaded him into the ambulance, I hopped over and crawled up in there beside him. He was still just screaming in pain. They put an oxygen mask on him and started checking his vital signs.

Luckily, we were only about a mile or two from the hospital, they got us there in like five minutes. I was still crying when we got to the hospital. They took off down the hall with Terry on the stretcher and disappeared around the corner. They took me off the other direction to x-ray my ankle. I thought they were taking him into the Operating Room for emergency surgery. In the x-ray room, while the guy was x-raying my ankle. I kept saying, "Where is Terry! Is he okay? Is he alive? Where is Terry?" The x-ray guy did not know anything.

After what seemed like forever, the doctor finally came in. He was holding my x-ray results and talking about my foot. I said, "I do not care about that! Where is Terry? Is he okay? Is he alive? Where is Terry?" He said, "Oh, they did not tell you? We sent him home, I could not find anything wrong with him." He said, "I think he just got the wind knocked out of him and it scared him." Man, was I relieved, I thought I had really killed him.

We got a good laugh out of it afterward. I went to court about a week later and found out that the lady who pulled out in front of us did not even have a driver's license. Another good life lesson learned at a young age for me, 'Be very careful on your bike'. Car drivers might not see you because your profile is so small, and they will pull right out in front of you! I have owned over forty bikes in my life and still love to ride. That is the only bike wreck I have ever been involved in. Thank God! I ride carefully though. I learned early how much it hurts to wreck your bike.

With so many more cars on the roadways today than there were in the '80s, it is even worse. So please be careful out there. Just slow down and increase your following distance. Be very aware of your surroundings and watch your blind spots, especially in the summertime, when there are a lot more motorcycles out on the roadways.

Chapter Seven

Just My Life

Dusty

When I was a teenager, I talked my mom into going in half with me and buying a horse. When I moved to my mom's house, she already had a horse. I wanted to get one so we could go riding together. That year when she got her tax returns, we bought a quarter horse named Dusty, for four hundred dollars. I paid two hundred, and she paid two hundred dollars. Dusty was a registered quarter horse, he had papers and everything. We got him cheap because a lady from our church was moving and just wanted him to go to a good home. He was a year and a half old and just barely broke. You talk about wild, Wow! What an animal.

I used to just sit out in our pasture brushing his hair and talking to him. It is funny how you can work out all of your problems talking to your horse, and he never even says a single word. I learned early that your horse is a good listener. He was a wild child though, sometimes when you wanted to go right, he wanted to go left, when you wanted to walk, he wanted to run! So, you had to be careful and he bucked me off more than once. He was a beautiful brown and white, rippling muscle, 'wild horse', and I loved him as I had never loved anything in my life. We were best friends from the very first moment, we could go anywhere together.

 I only rode with mom a few times though because she only rode in the pasture and down our road. Dusty and I wanted to go farther and farther. If you went west from mom's house, you were going to town. But if you went east, it was nothing but country and all dirt roads. Dusty and I always went farther and farther east. Two miles east of mom's house you would cross over I-35 and there were no more houses in sight. Dusty and I could ride forever with nothing but the wind at our backs: green grass in front of us and the beautiful sun setting behind us.

Sometimes I would take a canteen and we would ride all day. After riding all day and watching the sunset, I felt like an old cowboy. It was as if I had stepped back in time a hundred years, and it was just me and my horse. I am here to tell you, folks, I loved that horse, he was my best friend in the whole world. I have never been that close to an animal in my life. People say that dogs are "man's best friend." I believe that is because they have never owned a horse, Dusty was my best friend.

About a year later, one day while I was at school. I guess mom and her husband were broke as usual, they sold Dusty without even asking me. I guess he was half theirs, but I had spent the last year making him mine! It did not seem fair, I didn't even get to say goodbye. I do not have a picture or anything of him, my heart was broken.

All I have are my memories, and they can never

take those away. I bet they got three or four times what I had paid for him, but I would not have taken any amount of money for him, I loved that horse. At that time in my life, he was my most valuable possession. He is the only horse I have ever owned, I still miss him and wish I could go ride Dusty today. However, I never saw him again.

    I had a tough childhood, no matter how you slice it, but losing your best friend at such a young age is very hard on a kid. If I learned anything about parenting from my parents it was how not to treat your children. It has always been easy for me to be a single parent, in any situation just do the opposite of what my parents would have done:). I have always tried to lead by example and give my kids everything they need to be successful in life. They may not get everything they want, but they darn sure get everything they need. I also made sure they got to go to the same exact school from Pre-K to graduation, where they got to make lifelong friends. Instead of going to sixty or seventy different schools as I did, and moving around all the time.

Money Not Well Spent

When I was sixteen, my mom got arrested for writing hot checks around town. I remember the police coming to the house and hauling her away in handcuffs. Her two younger kids were screaming and crying and Sam the idiot was cussing and hollering at the police as they dragged her away. Wouldn't you know it, the idiot came straight to me. He knew I had been working hard and saving my money, and they were completely broke as usual. He put a huge guilt trip on me and tried to get me to pay the bail so she would not have to spend the night in jail. He said that they were broke and she had written a bunch of (hot checks) and he needed like seven hundred dollars to go bail her out. He knew I had about a thousand dollars in my savings account. I had been saving up for a new motorcycle.

After about an hour of his guilt trip and telling me about the horrible conditions in jail and how terrible of a son I was for not getting her out. I finally gave in, went to the bank, and withdrew my money. We then went and bailed her out. They promised to pay the money back, and they did. They gave me twenty or twenty-five dollars every payday (which was every two weeks) until I was paid back in full, this took about two years. Every time they gave me twenty dollars, I would put it in the gas tank of my truck or take Margaret out to eat or something, and I never really put the money back in my savings account.

At the end of the two years, it was as if the money had never existed at all. I always felt like I got screwed over on that deal because they took my life savings. I guess I am glad she did not have to spend the night in jail, but I still feel like I got screwed over. Another good life lesson learned for me at an early age though. I have never bounced a check, and I never will.

What an Idiot!

I will give you another example of Sam being an idiot. He and mom used to fight like cats and dogs, I have never seen anyone fight as they did. They were very religious and went to church every time the doors were open. Sam sang in the church choir and was even an elder in the church. Then, he would go home and cuss and scream and fight with his wife and kids like nothing you have ever seen. He and mom fought and argued all the time, usually about the bible.

They would get to screaming and cussing and arguing about each other's different interpretations of some scriptures. Many times, he would hit her upside the head with his bible or just throw it across the room at her. Mom liked to throw dishes, she broke every dish in the house at one time or another. She would throw plates and glasses or bowls or just any dish at him. From across the room or across the house.

Anyway, a couple of months after I moved out, I guess they got into a huge fight and she called 911. He was holding her and the kids at gunpoint and threatened to burn the house down! Someone called me and I went over there. They lived in the last house on a dead-end road. When I got there every cop in Guthrie was out there. They had the road closed at the end of the next block and were hollering at him on the bullhorn. They could not get him to answer the phone.

When I arrived, I talked to whoever was in charge. Once they realized I used to live there and I knew everyone in the house. They sent me up through the alley and around the back way to get the little old lady out of her house who lived next door. They were afraid of her getting caught up in any crossfire that may occur. They sent me because she knew me and they did not think she would answer the door for someone she didn't know. I sneaked around the back way and got her out through the alley, unbeknownst to anyone in Sam's house.

After a four-hour stand-off, the idiot finally came running out of his house. He was waving his gun around, screaming and cursing at the policemen. He tried to get in his truck and leave. About four cops tackled his dumb ass, cuffed him, and threw him in the back of a police car.

To this day I do not know why those cops did not shoot him when he came out waving his gun around. I guess it is because he never fired a shot. I give them credit though; they had a lot more restraint than I would have had. They sent him to the loony bin in Norman Oklahoma, where he spent three or four months in a padded room, then they let him go home. What an idiot!

Being Eighteen

My eighteenth year on earth was probably my

toughest one. Just before my eighteenth birthday, Margaret broke up with me. I got in a huge fight with the idiot and moved out of mom's house. I then went to town and rented an apartment. Somehow, I managed to get myself through my senior year of high school, I graduated completely on my own.

I also wrecked my motorcycle that year. I found out Christy was pregnant and I was having a baby. I needed to marry her and make things right with the baby. Mike closed the furniture store and I was out of a job, I needed a new one quickly. I got thrown out of the back of a pickup on a paved highway at 65 mph!

Yeah, you heard me right! We had been out hauling hay all day and half of the night. We were headed home from Dover Oklahoma, which is about thirty-five miles west of Guthrie. I had these two brothers helping me on the hay wagon. One of them had a little single cab short bed, S-10 pickup, we were headed home in that pickup.

The kid that owned the truck was driving, while his brother was lying in the bed asleep. The lady we had been working for was in the passenger's seat. I was sitting on the driver's side bed rails, in the back of the pickup looking over the cab and watching the road as he drove us home. We were all exhausted, and the lady in the cab was also asleep.

Then suddenly, as I was watching the road, we started veering over to the right side of the road across the white line! This is when I realized the kid driving had fallen asleep, also. It is funny looking back on it now, but at that point, I was the only person in the vehicle awake. I remember a few minutes earlier looking down through the back windshield, we were doing about 62 miles an hour. It all happened so fast, there was no time to react. Just as we veered off the right-hand side of the road into the grass, the kid driving suddenly woke up!

He was so scared and startled that he jerked the steering wheel too hard to the left. The vehicle went completely across the road and into the grass on the other side of the highway. At some point, he threw me over the side of the truck, I grabbed the side of the bed with my right arm. At this point, he was dragging me down the highway on my left side. It seemed like forever but was probably only a few seconds, I lost my grip and let go.

At that point, he ran over my left hand and forearm with the left rear tire of the truck. I bounced and did three or four somersaults and landed on the left shoulder of the highway. He finally got the truck to a stop about fifty yards down the road. He left a big skid mark and stopped sideways in the middle of the roadway.

They all jumped out and came running towards me. Just out of instinct I guess, as soon as I stopped tumbling, I jumped up and stood up. My whole left side, from my shoulder to my foot, was all torn up. My clothes were ripped up and all my skin was torn up with road rash. My left hand, which he ran over, was already starting to swell up. Blood was running down my left arm and hand, my head was bleeding from everywhere.

I guess every time I had somersaulted, I hit my head in a different spot on the highway. My head was bleeding from four to five places. When they got to me, I had already made a fist with my right hand. I was about to hit that kid who was driving and make sure he was awake! The problem was, I guess from the whole traumatic experience, I just fell back down. They all helped me to my feet and back into the truck. I got in on the passenger side and the two brothers got in the back of the truck. The lady drove us to the hospital, which was about thirty miles away.

It is funny because at that one moment I was the only one awake, but I am the only one who got hurt. At the hospital, I did not get a single stitch or have any broken bones. All they could do for me was clean my wounds. clean and wrap up all my road rash, and bandage my head, then they sent me home. I picked little pieces of rocks and gravel out of the sores on my head and left side, for weeks. I guess I am lucky to be alive, after being dragged down the highway at 62 miles an hour. I still have scars all over my left hand, forearm, head, and even a scar on my nose from this accident.

Man, was I young and naive, I settled out of court with the driver's insurance company, I did not even call a lawyer. I told them to pay my hospital bill and replace the boots, pants, and shirt that got destroyed as he dragged me down the highway and that would be good enough. They paid the hospital bill and gave me $200 for my boots, pants, and shirt. Lesson learned! I should have called a lawyer, right? Hell of a year, as I said, it is a wonder I survived.

Graduation

On the day Terry and I graduated from high school we got our picture in the paper. The day before graduation at rehearsal, the principal told us, "No sunglasses allowed at graduation." So, if you look at the graduation pictures or our picture in the paper you will see we are the two guys with shades on. The only ones in the whole crowd dumb enough to wear sunglasses after being told not to. We thought we were cool as we walked across the stage in our shades. We got chewed out later by the principal, but we made the paper:).

Chapter Eight

Growing up in a Small Town

Royal Rangers

As I said, mom and her family were very religious, we went to church all the time. Being in a small-town church, everybody knew everybody. So, rather than fight it and be a loner, I joined the Royal Rangers at an early age. Well for me it was an early age. But really at fourteen, I was one of the biggest kids in the class. Royal Rangers is the church's version of Boy Scouts. Being one of the bigger kids, the teacher depended on me to help some of the smaller kids quite a bit. I had a uniform with khaki pants and a dress shirt, with a cool bolo tie, and a beret hat.

As you complete different challenges, you got badges to sew on your chest or down your sleeve. We learned things like how to build a campfire, pitch a tent, bait a hook, and even shoot a black powder rifle and a bow and arrow. We also did arts and crafts things like woodworking and leatherworking. We took several bus trips to Colorado to go camping and fishing, we even learned how to cook over a campfire.

In case you have not figured it out yet, these were huge learning experiences for a teenage boy. Still, to this day, I lean on those experiences when I take my kids to the lake or fishing. I want them to experience nature as I did in the Royal Rangers. You should do the same for your children. There is nothing that compares to getting away from the city and breathing the clean air of Mother Nature while unplugging your kids from the Internet for a while. Try it!

Guthrie

Guthrie was Oklahoma's first state capital. In 1889 they had the "Land Run," where the government gave away free land, all you had to do was stake your claim, and it was yours. After the turn of the century, around 1902, some state legislatures and so-called lawmakers stole the state seal and took it to Oklahoma City, in the middle of the night. I guess they thought since it was called Oklahoma City it should be the state capital.

I often thought we should get a couple of guys and go steal it back, and see how they like that. Anyway, what this did was it threw Guthrie into a time lock, the town did not grow and no one moved there. Whereas Oklahoma City just got bigger and bigger. You know, being the state capital and all.

Guthrie just stayed the same and never changed. So nowadays, Guthrie is a huge tourist draw, all of the old Victorian-style buildings are still there, including old churches and houses. Most of which are bed and breakfasts these days. You can go to Guthrie and take the Trolley Tour and see all of the old houses and buildings while learning the entire history of Oklahoma. Today there are many antique shops and the Territorial

Museum, it is all about tourism.

Every April they celebrate the 89ers Days, with a week-long huge carnival and Saturday parade. The whole week is filled with entertainment like car shows, blue-ribbon pig events, and a rodeo. During the parade, a town that usually has thirteen thousand people in it will have as many as one hundred thousand showing up. At the end of the main street, which is also the end of the parade route, is the Masonic Temple. I have taken the tour, and it is an amazing building that takes up four city blocks. The Shriners are a huge part of the parade and are very entertaining.

As a teenager, I never missed the parade, I was always there with my friends. Margaret and I always went to the carnival, we enjoyed seeing the sites. One year I ate too much and puked on the Tilt-a-Whirl while it was spinning really fast and got about forty people wet. In later years I always took my kids to the parade, so they could experience the wonders of 89ers Days. If you get a chance, you should visit one day too.

Probably the biggest thing to happen in our small town, when I was a teenager, was the day Hollywood came to town. In 1987, when they were filming the movie *Rain Man*, with Tom Cruise and Dustin Hoffman, they spent about a week in downtown Guthrie. If you watched the movie there are about fifteen minutes with Tom Cruise and Dustin Hoffman with scenes in downtown Guthrie, Oklahoma. In the movie, they are supposed to be somewhere in Arizona or somewhere in a small town as they drive across the country, but it was filmed in Guthrie with all the old Victorian buildings downtown. If you know Guthrie you will recognize it easily. They had half of downtown blocked off for a week or so in 1987, and you could not go anywhere. I tried hard that week, but I never saw either of the two main characters in town. It sure caused an uproar around town though, everyone was talking about it all week long.

I really enjoyed living in a small town, everybody

knew me, and people would wave when they passed by on the street. Or say 'Hello,' when they saw me at the store, people were friendly and hospitable, they actually shook hands! Now I live in Oklahoma City and no one knows anyone, and they do not want to. They would rather run over you than have to wait for one minute for you to move, everyone is always in a hurry. They never slow down and enjoy life or stop and smell the roses. I still miss life in a small town.

Chapter Nine

The End of the Brown Beast!

I could write a whole other book about the 'Brown Beast.' I could tell you about how we used to race it down main street or how we used to tear up the back roads in it. Or all about tailgating out at the lake with your favorite girl. Or running from some kid that was chasing us because we "accidentally" bruised his Camaro getting out of Sonic.

Or about the time we went to the drive-in movies on Tuesday night and put 28 people in the back. Or about the time we were out joyriding in the middle of nowhere, ran out of gas, and had to walk eight miles back to town, (there were no cell phones in the 1980s.) But I cannot, because this is the story of the day we buried the Brown Beast! We laid her to rest.

When Terry was sixteen he got his first car, which was actually a truck, an ugly old brown Dodge pickup. I mean butt UGLY! It was the old square body, single cab, short bed, p.o.s. about a 1970 model and Terry loved that truck! He named it the "Brown Beast." He was so proud of that truck that his chest stuck out two feet. I believe he slept in it the first three nights, in his mom's driveway. It had an automatic transmission, with a V8 engine. It was so lightweight that it had more power and torque than you could hardly handle, and Terry drove the hell out of it!

He used to take the back way from his mom's house to the high school. On the west side of town, the last road on the north side of the main street is College Avenue. This is the back way so you did not have to go through the middle of town. College was far enough off the main street that you could just about go as fast as you wanted to and you would never see any cops back there.

Just past the river bridge and the railroad tracks,

right in front of the old furniture factory. There is a big hill in the middle of the road, like a giant speed bump. It is about fifteen feet tall and fifteen or twenty feet wide. You do not want to hit this hill at speeds over 20 mph or your front tires will come off of the ground! One day we were just out riding around and coming down College Avenue when Terry cocked the hammer on that old truck to see how fast she would run!

The police report said that we hit that hill at ninety miles an hour, were airborne for about thirty yards, and struck a telephone pole about halfway up and broke it off! The truck came crashing down to the ground with such force that Terry broke the steering wheel completely off with his chest. The kid in the middle smashed the windshield with his face, my door flew open and I landed out in the middle of a field. We did not wear seat belts in those days and cars did not have airbags. Somehow, by the Grace of God, none of us were seriously injured.

When we got back to Terry's house, he told his

mom that the throttle was stuck, and there was nothing that he could do. When actually, we had bet Terry that truck would not run a hundred and he was trying to prove us wrong. He kept the police report, it was proof it would run ninety. About a week later his mom got a bill in the mail from the City of Guthrie. It was for one telephone pole, ($750), man, was she pissed.

For the rest of Terry's life, he stuck to that story, that the throttle was stuck, because he was afraid his mom was going to give him a beating. Even years after she was dead, he still stuck to that story. If he was here right now, he would tell you that the throttle was stuck. Because he is still afraid that he is going to get a beating from his mom, and that was the end of the 'Brown Beast.'

For the rest of Terry's life every time he talked about the 'Brown Beast,' or the words 'Brown Beast' were mentioned he would always put his right hand over his heart as a show of respect. Even at Terry's funeral, the preacher told the entire audience, at Terry's request, "If anybody in here utters the words 'Brown Beast,' everyone in here has to put their right hand over their heart." Man, he loved that truck.

I hope you guys have fond memories of your first car. Terry and I had some of the greatest times of our lives in those old trucks. You can take a lot of things away from a guy, but you are well warned to not try and take his truck. Some of my best memories are of just us two guys in a truck. With the whole world in front of our windshield, and nothing but time to kill.

Terry's Hay-Hauling Career

All the way through my teenage years I worked on the hay wagon every summer for Randy. We were constantly looking for help, we could not keep hands. They would work for one hour and then start complaining that it was too hot or the hay bales were too heavy, and they would go home. Sometimes, we would go through three or four guys in one day. So, I was constantly asking guys at school if they wanted to work. One day I asked Terry if he wanted to work and make some extra money. He was like, "Hell yeah! Let's go make some money!", he was all gung-ho.

So, I loaded him up after school and we took off to the hayfield. We were only there for about ten minutes when he started complaining that it was too hot. The bales were too heavy, and the work was too dirty and nasty. I said, "Just hang in there, go get a drink of water." So, we got back to work, and about ten minutes later he said, "Man, I don't know if I can do this." I said, "Come on man, just make it through today. You can make $100 today, and I need the help." We went back to work and he was moving really slow, looking like he was about to have a heat stroke. He dropped to one knee, looked up at me, and said. "Oh man, I forgot my inhaler! You are going to have to take me home!" (You cannot make this stuff up. That is exactly what he said.) I still laugh every time I think about it.

I forgot to tell y'all when we were teenagers, Terry had "asthma." It was not a problem 99 percent of the time, but it would act up really badly from time to time. Usually when he was trying to get out of doing something. He never carried an inhaler with him... So, I took him home and that was the end of Terry's hay-hauling career, which lasted probably less than thirty minutes.

It is a good thing that boy went to college and got an education because he was not cut out for manual labor. But I wouldn't trade those memories for the world. Thanks for trying buddy.

Chapter Ten

Christy, Baby Melissa, and I

Melissa

Christy was not my high school sweetheart. Margaret left just before my eighteenth birthday. A couple of months later, I got into it with the "idiot," moved to town, and got my own apartment. I let a kid from school move in with me and pay half the bills. The problem was when the bills came, he never had his half. After about three short months, I had to dissolve our partnership so to speak, I kicked his ass out! During those three months, his girlfriend was at our apartment a lot, and her best friend was Christy.

So, Christy and I started dating, probably from peer pressure. The very first time we had sex she got pregnant! Again, I was naive, I had only had sex with one other person in my life, I had never even had a condom on before. Looking back, I really did not know Christy very well, we had only been dating for a couple of weeks, we certainly were not in love. I remember going over to Christy's parent's house to pick her up for a date one evening. Her mom answered the door and said, 'Hello Daddy!' That is how I found out that she was pregnant.

    Her parents told me that it was not going to be a shotgun wedding. If I did not want to marry her, they would take care of Christy and the baby. I thought about it for a long time, because I knew we were not in love. After Margaret left, I had already been talking with the Army Recruiter at the high school. I planned to join the Army, get on the G. I. Bill, and go to college, but after a lot of thought and soul searching. I decided the best thing to do was to get married and have the baby. Again, taking responsibility for my actions as I had always done, so we got married.

    Melissa was born in February 1988, I was a proud poppa, she was the cutest baby I had ever seen. I passed out cigars to all my friends the next day. Christy almost died giving birth though. It was a small-town hospital and they are not really equipped for anything unusual that may go wrong. I guess her being a teenager and pretty small down there, they could not get the baby out, and it was taking way too long. After about an hour, Christy had passed out from all the intense labor and trying to push the baby out, she was exhausted.

I could tell by the look on the doctor's face that he was scared and not sure what to do when she passed out and could no longer "push." I was standing right beside Christy when he sprang into action because he knew that he was about to lose the baby and possibly even the mother. He yelled, "Get out of my way!" to the nurse. Then he grabbed a big pair of scissor-looking things and made a large cut on each side where the baby's head would come out.

After what seemed like forever, he pulled the baby out and had me cut the umbilical cord. It took a while for the nurse to clean the baby's airway and get her breathing, but I knew she was fine when I heard her screaming and crying. They handed her to me to hold for the first time, you should have seen the smile on my face!

Then, all of a sudden the nurse said, "I can not find a pulse!" Christy had lost so much blood from the doctor cutting her that she did not have a pulse and was about to die. She had been unconscious for a long time while they got the baby out. The doctor said, "Everyone out!", and they cleared the room.

A few minutes later a nurse came out and asked me to sign some papers so they could give her blood. I remember signing the papers, and they said that if she died the hospital was not responsible, because they had done everything they could to try and save her. I asked the nurse if she was going to be okay. The nurse just looked up to the sky, as if to say "Pray," and went back into the room.

I thought she was dying, and like I said we were not in love, but she was the mother of my child and I didn't want her to die. I remember going into the bathroom so I could be alone. Christy has a big family and they were all there. I prayed, "God, please don't let her die. Please! I need her to help me raise this baby. I cannot do it alone. Please!" I walked back to the waiting room with tears rolling down my cheek, where everybody was waiting.

Just as I walked in the nurse came in the other door and said, "She is awake if you want to see her?" I have never been real religious or believed in the power of prayer, but that was a miracle as far as I am concerned. They were all but pronouncing her dead thirty minutes ago.

We named the baby Melissa, Christy did not want the baby though, she did not want to take care of her. She did not want the responsibility. She did not like going to school and people knowing that she had a baby at home. She was a year behind me in school.

When Melissa was born, Christy was still in high school. She tried to get me to give the baby to her parents. But I said, "No way! She is my kid, and I will take care of her!" Christy and I fought a lot, not only over the baby but also about money and responsibility. You have to pay your bills and your rent, we were only teenagers, but I was an adult.

We had rented a house from Terry's mom, and we had bills to pay! Mike closed the furniture store during my senior year, after working for him for three years, I now had to find a new job. I went to work at Guthrie Green House and made minimum wage ($3.35 an hour) doing general labor.

They later made me spray man, which meant I sprayed pesticides, and I got $3.50 an hour. This meant after taxes I would barely bring home $100 a week. Since Terry's mom charged us $150 a month for rent, I had to save up all month to pay for it. After buying groceries and paying utilities there was not much left, so I saved what was left all month for the rent.

Here is the problem though, Christy loved to play bingo. She loved to go play the gambling machines out at the VFW. She was constantly taking the money I was saving for rent and going to bingo with it, (She knew where I hid it). So we fought and fought and fought. Pretty soon, I had all I could take and was ready for a divorce.

I loved Melissa and enjoyed playing with her and taking care of her. I knew Christy did not want her, she had made it more than clear. However with me gone, they would move to Christy's parent's house, and they were good people. I knew Melissa would be safe there and well taken care of. So, I filed for divorce and my marriage was over. You talk about 'tough', you should try being a teenage father, with a new wife and baby and surviving on $3.35 an hour. With a wife who loves to drink and gamble and does not want to help you take care of the baby. Try it, I dare you! It is a lot of fun! I did it for almost eight years.

I think Christy hated me because I took away her teenage years and she loved to drink and party with her friends in high school, but she couldn't, with a baby at home. As I look back on my life, I do not believe I would change anything I did in those early years, (Except), I would try to get full custody of Melissa. Her mother did not want her, and after I left, her Grandparents ended up raising her, while Christy ran around. I should have been there for her. Just FYI you guys, daughters need dads too.

I always tell my sister that on judgment day, when I am standing before God and he asks me why I did this or why I did that with my life. My answer will always be, "Sir, I did the very best I could with what you gave me to work with. Which were my two hands and my little naive brain. The rest I had to improvise."

Chapter Eleven

The Werewolf Story

Baker's Lake

When we were in high school, we used to spend a lot of hot summer evenings out at Baker's Lake. It was private property but we did not care. Where the bridge crosses the southwest corner of the lake, it is far enough away from the people's house that they cannot see you. On hot summer days, there would be fifteen or twenty kids out there jumping off the bridge into the water. It is about a twenty-foot drop and it was a blast. The cops would not usually bother us because Baker's Lake is just outside the city limits.

People would park their cars along the side of the road and crank up their stereo. Then we would take turns jumping off the bridge into the lake. One day, about three people before Terry's and my turn to jump, a kid jumped and hit something in the water. He came up screaming for help! A couple of guys on the bank jumped in and helped him to shore. He was screaming in agony and blood was running down both of his legs as they dragged him out of the water. Terry and I ran down to see if we could help. The kid's legs were both cut up real bad, from his ankles to his thighs. We helped them get him to a car and someone ran him to the hospital.

I was told later that he got several hundred stitches. You could not see anything in the murky water, but after further inspection, someone said that there were some old rusted fifty-gallon barrels down there that the kid had probably hit. We never jumped off of Baker's Lake bridge again! Lesson learned. Thank you, Lord, I dodged another bullet.

Best Fishing Hole Ever!

As I said, farm ponds were our favorite place to fish and we did not ask permission. We just jumped over the fence and went fishing. There was this fishy-looking pond about two miles south of my mom's place that I had been wanting to fish for like a year. The problem was every time I drove by, there seemed to be a car in the driveway and someone home. There were "No Trespassing" signs posted all along the fence, but man, this place really looked good. There were trees all around, which was very secluded. You know the type where you can just tell by looking that it is a good fishing hole.

Anyway, one day Terry and I drove by and there were no cars there. I do not know if they finally went on vacation or what, but we were going fishing regardless. I did not want to park my truck right in front of their house, just in case they came home, right? So, I parked about half a mile up the street. We grabbed our poles and walked down there and jumped over the fence. This was some of the best fishing I have ever experienced in my life! We were catching huge bass and crappies, (Fish On!), on every cast. In about twenty minutes we had a stringer full of fish as long as your arm.

We decided to walk around the pond and try the other side, I went to the left and Terry to the right. We caught some little ones, but nothing to write home about as we walked around. We passed each other on the other side and continued back to where we had started.

We were dreaming about the fish fry we were going to have when we got home. Just as we got back to where my stringer was anchored in the ground. We saw this giant, I mean huge, head of a snapping turtle sticking out of the water. And he's got the last one of those fish in his mouth just gulping it down! This turtle was as big as one of the tires on my truck. We started throwing rocks at him and screaming, but it was too late! He had eaten our fish dinner, right before our eyes.

I love to fish and take my kids all the time, but as an adult, I have never kept the fish and cleaned them as I did in my teenage years. Today I am a catch-and-release kind of guy. If I want a fish dinner, I just go to Long John Silver's. I have often wondered if that is not because that giant turtle ate our fish dinner that day. I felt so bad for those poor fish stuck on that stringer with no way to escape.

There Are Werewolves in Those Woods!

This was always Terry's favorite story, he loved to tell it. It would make him laugh and cry, practically at the same time. If he were here today, I believe he would tell it exactly like this. Enjoy!

When I was in high school, I drove an old Chevy pickup, I carried a .22 rifle behind the seat, and I always had my fishing pole with me! If we saw a place where we wanted to fish, we just jumped over the fence and went fishing. We did not ask permission or Google the answer, we just jumped over the fence. We have been shot at, dogs sicced on us, and ran off of more places than I can tell you. One evening just before dark, we were out running the back roads, looking for a place to shoot our guns. I am not exactly sure where we were, all I know is that we were on an old dirt road about six or eight miles west of town, out in the middle of nowhere.

Anyway, we soon came upon this place that looked promising. It was a huge wooded lot with trees on all four sides and a big clearing out in the center, with an old pump jack or oil well site on it. There were not any houses around. There was one of those big galvanized stockade gates, with four or five rails on it. I looked at Terry and said, "Let's check it out." I parked the truck as far off the road as I could get. There is really no shoulder on those narrow dirt roads. I told him to check the gate and I would get my rifle from behind the seat. He had his grandpa's old pistol with him.

He ran down to the gate and hollered, "It's locked." I ran down and sure enough, there was a big chain going through the gate and around the post, with a big padlock on it. We just looked at each other and smiled. Hell, they were practically inviting us in, they put up a gate that had rail steps on it like a ladder. This was the easiest fence we had ever jumped over.

We climbed over and started walking down towards that old wellhead, it was about two hundred yards away. It was just about dark; we were trying to hurry so we could get in some good target practice before dark. We did not even have a flashlight with us. (I do not recommend doing this to you kids today!), but we shot everything you could shoot at on that wellhead. We shot out the sight glass and blasted the hell out of the radiator.

Then we started just shooting into the tree line on the back side of this property. I would say, "I bet you can't hit that tree" and he would shoot. Then he would say, "I bet you can't hit that one" and I would shoot. Then we would trade guns and do the whole thing over again. All of a sudden we heard this very loud high-pitched squealing sound coming from the tree line. We just froze with fear and looked at each other in complete terror, with eyes as big as saucers, shaking in our boots! You could hear this thing screaming and it sounded like it was getting closer and closer and closer! We did not say anything, we both just turned and headed for my truck as fast as we could run!

You could hear something running in the woods behind us, and it was screaming in this high-pitched squeal. It was an ear-piercing, blood-curdling, crying noise, and we were absolutely scared to death! I was running as fast as I could but it was dark and I could not see anything. We were running through heavy brush and tall grass, with tree limbs scratching us and tripping over limbs and twigs and rocks. We could hear this thing running behind us, just screaming and howling at us!

We got to the gate at the same time and both jumped up on it, and I guess just from our momentum, it swung open! (This is a true story, I was there and it happened just like this.) Now, we had both checked that gate not twenty minutes earlier and I would swear on my daddy's grave that it was locked!

Again, we did not say anything, we just looked at each other in utter terror and complete bewilderment that this gate could somehow be unlocked. We jumped off the gate and ran to the truck as fast as we could run! I still remember the look on Terry's face when we got to the truck. His eyes were the size of baseballs, and he was white as a ghost, he was absolutely scared to death! We did not say anything all the way back to town. I drove as fast as that old truck would run. I was shaking so badly; that I could barely shift gears.

I dropped him off at his house and I went home. It was not until I got home that the reality and nightmare hit me. What had we shot? Who else may have been out there or seen us? Did we just shoot someone's cow or donkey? Maybe it was a mythical creature, like Bigfoot or Sasquatch. I think I was just as scared afterward not knowing what, or who we may have shot as I was when I was running for my life from that screaming beast.

Over the next few days, we talked about it a lot.

Terry always thought it was a werewolf, I thought it sounded like a baby screaming, but way too loud! I am not sure what it was, I never saw it in the dark! Maybe a horse, a moose, a unicorn, I really do not know! All I know is that we injured something in the woods that night. It charged at us from out of that tree line and ran us out of the woods and scared the life out of us!

Remember earlier when I said I was scared to death that first day of junior high school? That was nothing compared to how scared I was the night that werewolf chased us out of the woods. Still today that is the most scared, by far, that I have ever been in my entire life. I can assure you we never went back to that property again, private property or not. They could have been holding a city-wide party there, but there is no way you could have ever gotten us to go back in there again...

And that, my friends, is the werewolf story.

Chapter Twelve

A Different World

My dad taught me, just like his dad had taught him, and his dad before him, that you always carry your pocket knife in your pocket, Period! I could write a whole other book on the reasons why. If you are a guy who carries one you know exactly what I am talking about, it is like a "multitool" for life! Everything from trimming your fingernails to cutting up your lunch. Loosen a bolt, cut a rope, pick your teeth, or even in a pinch defend yourself or your loved ones. The uses are absolutely endless.

My dad would have never left the house without his, and he taught me the same. My dad gave me my first pocket knife when I was six years old, I remember it like it was yesterday. It made me feel like a man! It was an (Old Timer) with three blades, it was brand new and shiny. I thought it was made of solid gold. There is no way I would have left home without it. I even slept with it under my pillow for like a year.

When I was in school, I always had my pocket knife with me, as far back as I can remember, even in grade school. I did not try to hide or conceal it! I always had it out using it for something and nobody cared.

When I was in the ninth grade, one morning just before school started. I was standing on the sidewalk talking with my friends. I had my knife out cleaning or trimming my fingernails when I accidentally dropped the knife. Just as I reached down to pick it up a girl walked by and stepped on it, with my right index finger caught under the blade. She literally cut the end of my finger practically off! it was just before the first knuckle. The end of my finger was cut like three-fourths of the way through and was just barely hanging on. As you know with your fingertips, it bled profusely.

I ran into the office, with blood all over my hand and running down my arm. The lady at the desk yelled,

"Oh, my God!" They wrapped it up with some cloth and tape, and one of the ladies in the office ran me to the hospital. One of them called my mom because she met us at the hospital. The stitches did not hurt, but the deadening shots, at the end of your fingertips, were extremely excruciating and I screamed in pain!

It took like eight stitches to put the end of my finger back on, I still have the scar. For the rest of high school, every time I saw that girl, I would not say anything. I would just growl and make a mean face. Lesson learned... Never pick your knife up by the blade, especially if some girl is walking by:).

Could you imagine if my fourteen-year-old son took a pocket knife to school today? He would be expelled for a year. It would be all over the news that he is a terrorist or something... A different world.

When I was seven, I used to ride my bike down to the corner store and buy cigarettes for my stepmom. She smoked Marlboro Lights 100s, I still remember because I went every day and they cost .79 cents a pack. I have never smoked, but I believe today they are over five dollars a pack. Can you even imagine a 7-year-old in a store buying cigarettes today? How funny... A different world.

In high school and junior high, we had a designated smoking area for staff and students. In 1981 when I started at Guthrie Junior High School, they had a smoking lounge for the teachers. Today, you can't even smoke on the entire campus in most schools. Again, I have never smoked, but it just seems like we are losing our freedom. I never had a problem with them smoking outside, Did you?

I guess I am just old school, at least my kids think so! I still watch M*A*S*H, Gunsmoke, and The Rifleman. I tell my kids if they pay attention, they will find a good life lesson in every episode. They do not make TV like that anymore! I am so old that I can remember no cell phones, no computers or internet, even no microwaves, no DVD players or VHS, and no remote-controlled TV, you had to get up and walk to the TV to change the channel. Remember when the TV went off after the late news and you knew it was bedtime? Or gas, when I got my motorcycle license at age fourteen, gas was .89 cents a gallon... A different world.

Nowadays, kids completely depend on the Internet for everything. From homework to video games to movies to music to "How do I shave for the first time?" or "How far is it to the moon?" It is too easy. They do not have to really know anything to survive. It is all right there for the asking. They do not have to ask their parents anything, except "What time is dinner?" They just Google everything they want to know, it is too easy... A different world.

In the eighth grade, I joined the wrestling team. I tried to get Terry to wrestle but his most athletic moves were on the square dance floor. Later when we went to the ninth grade, surprisingly, my wrestling coach was Mr. Scott, our seventh and eighth-grade music teacher's husband. I liked Mr. Scott, just as I did his wife.

I used to go to his house on weekends and during the summer, he would give me the keys to the high school so I could go work out. I could get into the gym, wrestling room, weight room, and anywhere I wanted to go. Can you imagine if a coach gave a ninth-grade student the keys to the whole schoolhouse these days? Funny right? He would be fired just for thinking about it. I tell my kids that I grew up in a different world than theirs. In high school, we had a designated smoking area for staff and students to use, just outside the back door. Can you imagine that today?

When I was in the eighth grade on the wrestling team, I lost seven pounds in one day, one time. The wrestling coach got me out of all my classes that day and had me run all day. I needed to lose seven pounds so I would not have to wrestle as a heavyweight. We had a wrestling match that evening against Kingfisher, a rival town. I had already lost about a month earlier to a giant black kid they had, and I did not want to wrestle him again! The only way for me to not wrestle him was to get under 180, and I needed to lose seven pounds to do this.

Coach got me excused from all my classes that day, and he gave me salt tablets to take to make me sweat. He would not let me eat anything all day. All I could do was run and drink water. I took salt tablets and ran on the track all day, we did not have a sauna to set in. At the end of the school day, I had lost almost eight pounds. I did not eat anything all day until after the weigh-in. Then, the coach gave me a power bar or something just before my match. I won that match and pinned the smaller, weaker kid easily. I was so glad I did not have to wrestle that giant black kid again.

Can you imagine if a coach took a kid out of school all day and gave him salt tablets so he would sweat and made him run all day to lose weight? In today's world that coach would be fired for inhumane practices and child abuse, or stunting the kid's growth...

A different world, I tell you.

Later, when I went to the ninth grade my wrestling career soon ended. In high school, we had a kid named Brian who was a state champion wrestler three years in a row. Brian was a tall skinny kid, and I could never figure out how he could beat me or pin me so easily. I guess it is because he had been wrestling since he was a toddler and he was now state champion.

Anyway, every day after school at wrestling practice, the coach would make me and Brian wrestle in front of the entire wrestling class. Brian would use me as a wrestling dummy, he pinned me in like five seconds. I was bigger and stronger, but the coach would say, "Now watch, it does not matter how big your opponent is. If you practice these moves you can out-wrestle anybody." He was right, Brian would pin me again and again and again. Pretty soon I realized I should be at work, instead of down in the wrestling room being a wrestling dummy for Brian to practice on:)

Chapter Thirteen

Just the Way I am Built

You probably figured out by now that I grew up and matured at a very early age. Everything from my terrible childhood to getting my first job at thirteen to getting a girl pregnant at eighteen and the responsibilities of becoming a father. All these things made me a very trustworthy, mature, and responsible person, at a young age. Terry's mom knew it when I was just thirteen. Mike at the furniture store could see it when I was only fifteen, Randy could see it every day on the hay wagon. Gale, who hired me at the greenhouse and later bumped me up to spray man could see it and so on and so on.

Terry had a younger brother, Kenny, whom I was always bailing out of trouble. You see every time there was a serious problem in their family, Terry or his mother called me. Terry's mom knew that she could always count on me to do the right thing. She knew that I did not drink, do drugs, smoke, or get into trouble. She knew that I went to church, tried to live my life right, and was very responsible with my actions. She knew she could depend on me. She knew every time those boys went anywhere or did anything, if I was with them they would be fine.

Every time there was a major problem, she knew that she could count on me to help solve it. For example, if one of them was in a fender bender or in the hospital for some reason. She would call me, to see if I could help. Or if her car was not running right, she would call me to look at it. Or if her washing machine broke or a thousand other things, she always thought of me first to see if I could help. I bailed those boys out of more trouble when we were teenagers than I can even remember.

Like the time Terry got into a huge fight at school with a kid, he had been friends with for years. They were going to settle it after school in the park. Terry's mom somehow found out through the grapevine that Terry and this kid were going to fight that evening at the park.

Rather than trying to talk Terry out of it, because she knew it would not work anyway. She called me and asked me to try and talk some sense into him before he got hurt or arrested for fighting. Or at least she asked for me to be there and make sure he did not get hurt. Terry was pretty scrappy in his teenage years and if you pushed him, you would be riding the short bus the rest of the year! And this kid had pushed him to his limit.

So, I went to the park that evening. His mom didn't know it, but I was planning on going anyway, because I had Terry's back, just as he had my back many times before. It was a pretty good fight, it lasted a while, they both got knocked down and wrestled around for quite a while. Terry got some bumps and bruises but was not hurt too bad. I am not sure anybody really won, I was there and had his back though, just to make sure no one else jumped in.

There was also the time when Kenny, Terry's younger brother, was going to shoot himself. Because "life was too hard" or he had just had too much to drink. Either way, Terry's mom called me to see if I could defuse the situation before she called the cops as a last resort. Kenny was sitting down on the dead-end of a dirt road by the railroad tracks. He was just sitting there in his car, about half-drunk, and had a .22 pistol in his hand. He would not let Terry or his mom come close to the car. Every time they tried, he threatened to shoot them or himself.

I had traded him that gun about a year earlier for some tools or something. Not because I needed the tools, but because he liked and wanted the pistol really bad, and he was my friend, and I did not really need the gun, so I traded him. However, here we are a year later and he is about to kill himself with my gun! I walked down to his car real slow and told him it was me. I said, "Don't shoot!" I walked up and sat down in the passenger seat.

It took me about an hour to talk him out of killing himself. I told him he had everything to live for, and he was young and had his whole life ahead of him. I told him it did not matter what crap he was going through at school or with his parents, it was not worth killing yourself. Then I said "It will all pass soon, and you will be old enough to get your own place. So then nobody can boss you around or tell you what to do." I was not about to let him shoot himself, or anyone else for that matter, with my gun.

After about an hour he handed me the gun, I think we were both in tears as we walked back towards his mom. The next day I took the gun to the pawnshop and gave him the money. He probably was not old enough for the gun in the first place. I learned responsibility for my actions at an early age. I try to instill some of these values in my children as I watch them grow into young adults, I hope you do the same.

Chapter Fourteen

My House Burned Down!

Rock Concert

When I was fifteen, I took a field trip with our Church Youth Group to Tulsa Oklahoma, to see a Petra concert, Petra was a Christian Rock Band. I heard some of their music, and it sounded a lot more like rock and roll than church hymns. The youth pastor drove the church bus with about thirty kids on it. Tulsa is about a hundred miles northeast of Oklahoma City, I remember being excited to go. We left about noon on Saturday, even though the concert was not until later that evening. It would take the pastor about an hour and a half to drive the bus to Tulsa. Plus we were going to stop about halfway and eat lunch.

Then, when we got to Tulsa we were supposed to walk around downtown and see the sights before going to the concert. Everything went smoothly on the takeoff, he got us all loaded onto the bus and headed up the highway. That old bus did not move very fast, and it seemed like it took forever. I was happy when we got to the halfway point and stopped for a lunch break at a small-town pizza joint. We were at the pizza place for probably about an hour. When everybody was fed, some of us boys went to the game room in the back and played Pac-Man or something. While some of the other kids went outside to goof around.

After about ten minutes in the game room, I looked up from the machine I was playing and did not see anybody I recognized in the game room. So, I thought they must be getting ready to leave. I walked out into the main part of the restaurant and again did not see anybody I recognized. Then, I hurried past the people in the restaurant and ran out the door to get on the bus. To my surprise though, the bus was already gone and nowhere in sight! No one had told me it was time to go, I did not hear anything. But somehow, they had left me at the pizza place!

I guess the youth pastor had miscounted when he did a headcount. I ran back into the restaurant, I went up to the cashier lady and told her my bus had left without me. I said, "What do I do?" She went and got the manager. Again, we did not have any cell phones in the 1980s. You could not just call the pastor and have him turn around. The pastor told me that he was driving for almost thirty minutes. When another kid, the one sitting beside me on the bus I think, came up and told him that I was missing. Then he had to turn around and drive all the way back.

In the meantime, the manager had tried calling my mom but got no answer. He tried calling our church back in Guthrie but got no answer also, it was Saturday! They then called the police, who were there when the bus finally pulled back into the pizza parking lot. Man, was I embarrassed and relieved at the same time. The pastor turned around and drove back to Tulsa, we made it to the concert on time.

We were only at the concert for about fifteen minutes, I think, and the band had only played two songs. There was a strong smell of marijuana coming from all around us, and you could even see several people smoking it. The youth pastor loaded us all right back onto the bus and drove an hour and a half back to our church in Guthrie. When I got home that day, I was exhausted, it seemed like a total waste of a Saturday. I said to mom, "I told you that it was a hard rock band, and people smoke weed at rock concerts." There were many, many life lessons I learned that day, my friends.

Where There's Smoke, There's Fire!

When I was nineteen, just a few months after my daughter Melissa was born, I burned our house down. At that time, we were renting a house on the west side of town from Terry's mother. One fine spring day, I was off work because I had a dentist appointment that morning. I used to buy old cars and motorcycles and fix them up in my spare time to try and make extra money. For the past week or two, I had been rebuilding an engine on our back porch. Like a goober, I was using gasoline to clean the parts, it was the only thing I had that was strong enough to get the grease off.

I do not remember now which part I was working on at the time, I believe it was one of the heads. I had it all cleaned with gas and wiped it down with an old rag. Just to make sure it was clean, I decided to take it to the bathtub and rinse it off. I took it to the bathroom and laid it in the bathtub, I went back outside to get some rags or something.

I was only gone for two or three minutes, when I came back the entire bathroom was engulfed in flames! I froze in a panic! Then suddenly, I just started stomping at it and throwing everything I could grab at it trying to put it out, but it was too late. It was already out of control and spreading to the living room and back bedroom. Luckily, we lived right behind the fire station on the west side of town.

Guthrie has two fire departments. One was on the east side of town and another one was caddy cornered on the block right in front of my house on the west side of town. If you walked out of my front door and looked to your right, you would see the back of their building.

With no time to lose, because my house is burning down. I ran across the street into the firehouse yelling, "Fire! Fire! My house is on fire!" I did not see anybody. I ran into the office yelling, "Fire! Fire!" I ran into the bathroom yelling. Then I ran upstairs yelling, "Fire! Fire!" There was nobody in sight. The whole freaking building was empty with not a soul anywhere.

I ran back outside and stopped a lady who was driving down the road and told her to go call 911, "My house is on fire!" About twenty minutes later as I am standing in the front yard in tears, helpless to do anything. The fire department from the east side of town finally arrives on the scene. By the time they got there, the flames were shooting out the top of our house. The whole house was on fire! Now that I look back, I thank God that I was the only one home that day. Christy had taken baby Melissa to her mother's house for the day.

I did not know it, because it was hot outside that day and there were not any heaters on in our house. However, the wall furnace inside the wall between our bathroom and the living room must have had a pilot light burning inside it that caused the fire and ignited the gas in the bathtub. And just my luck, the west side fire department had set an old house on fire that day out in the country that needed to be burned up. They were out there practicing putting it out. Again, there were a number of life lessons learned that day my friends.

I got a new job out of it though. Terry's mom took the insurance money and rebuilt the house, putting me on the payroll, I helped Terry's dad rebuild that entire house. Then a year later Christy, baby Melissa and I moved back in.

Chapter Fifteen

Our Trip to Atlanta and the Georgia Dome

Georgia on My Mind

When I was nineteen, Terry talked me into joining Amway, he got in through a lady he worked with. The biggest part of Amway is for you to get more people to sign up, then you make money off of everyone under you that you convince to join. It took him a month to get me to sign up, I finally got it though. If I could make five cents on every roll of toilet paper sold in Oklahoma City, I would be a millionaire. They have hundreds of products; toilet paper is just an example, but I understood the concept and joined up.

Just after I joined, they were about to have the largest Amway convention in history, in the Georgia

Dome, in Atlanta Georgia. It was a three-day event that went on for twenty-four hours straight each day. With dozens of guest speakers and live entertainment, live bands, and even comedians. There were over one hundred thousand people in the Georgia Dome each day. It was the biggest and craziest thing I had ever seen in my nineteen years.

It took us sixteen hours to drive out there. We drove Terry's ugly Ford Ranger pickup that he had after the "Brown Beast" died. We left early one morning from Terry's house, around 4 a.m. Terry would drive first. However, Terry hated to drive and normally would fall asleep if he had to drive very far. We were drinking coffee and talking to each other, I figured he would be okay for a while.

Terry used to work in Ponca City, which is 100 miles north of Guthrie. He worked in a clinic where he took x-rays. He would get his forty hours in over the weekend. He worked straight through from Friday night to Monday morning, then he would drive home. They had a cot in the back room. If there were no x-rays to take, he could take a nap once in a while during that forty-hour stretch. He told me that after work he was so tired that most of the time he did not even remember driving home. He used to say, "I've driven farther asleep than most people have awake."

So, after about an hour he was done driving and it was my turn. I drove for fourteen hours straight. We were trying to hurry so we would not be late for the opening ceremonies. One of our favorite speakers, someone high up in Amway, was scheduled to speak first and we did not want to miss it. I kept asking him if he wanted to drive but he always had some excuse. Like he was reading the map, or he would drive after lunch or something, but he never drove.

We got lost in Atlanta trying to find the hotel. This was the largest city we had ever seen, but we got there in plenty of time before the convention started. We went to the hotel to check-in and find our room first. I was exhausted from the drive and wanted to sleep. We had about four hours to get some sleep before we needed to go. Terry had made the arrangements for the room and said it was the only room available in the whole city. We got our room key and went upstairs.

As soon as we walked in, I could see there was a problem. It was one small room with one full-size bed and a small loveseat in the corner. I looked at him and said, "Where am I supposed to sleep? I am not sleeping with you!" He said, "It is the only room that was available, we will have to make do." He crawled into the bed, while I grabbed a pillow and sat down on the loveseat.

I tried to sleep because I was exhausted from driving the last fourteen hours straight. But I could not get comfortable. I could not stretch out on the loveseat and had to try and sleep all curled up or with my legs dangling off the other end of the armrest, it was very uncomfortable. I did not get thirty minutes of sleep, before you knew it, it was time to go. We left his truck at the hotel.

The Georgia Dome was only a few blocks away. It would give us time to see the city a little bit if we walked over to the Dome. This city was huge and there was way too much traffic. We had never seen anything like it, growing up in a small town. As we walked to the Dome, we never thought this many people even existed on earth. That first day just over one hundred thousand people showed up, it was unbelievable! We enjoyed it though, with all the speakers, comedians, live music and entertainers, it was awesome!

We stayed all day, until way after dark. We were so tired that we could hardly walk. It was four or five blocks back to the hotel. By the time we got to the hotel, it was almost midnight. I had been awake for most of the last forty-eight hours and was totally exhausted. However, I was staring at that love seat again. The only choice was to sleep with Terry or try the love seat again, the love seat it was! I might have slept for two hours that night, but because I was so tired, it did not matter what position I was in. We got up early before seven in the morning. I woke up with a crick in my neck and back and really my whole body. We got something to eat and walked back to the convention.

The second and third days were the same as the first had been, just with different speakers and entertainers. We stayed and watched just about all of it each day until we could not stay awake any longer. Then we would walk to the room, get a little bit of sleep and come back the next morning. We really enjoyed it, there were lots of motivational speakers, singers, and entertainers.

After three days of it though, we were worn out and ready to head home. Terry drove first, just as he had when we left Guthrie. I was as exhausted as I had ever been in my life. Three days on that love seat had just about killed me! I bet I didn't sleep six hours the whole time we were there. Usually, I cannot sleep while someone else is driving, it is just a phobia of mine.

However, I was so tired that ten minutes in I started dozing off and closed my eyes. You know how when your head falls over to one side, and it startles you awake because you are trying to stay awake? I did that two or three times and the third time it startled me awake, I noticed that the white line, which was supposed to be on the right side of the highway, was in the middle of the hood of Terry's pickup. I looked over at Terry and he was completely asleep. I grabbed the wheel and yelled, "Wake up man! Wake up!" Then I drove fourteen hours straight to get us home.

We stopped somewhere in Mississippi, Terry brought with him our fake IDs which I thought his mom had destroyed, he said that he found them in a kitchen drawer. We went into a titty bar/gambling casino in Mississippi that was nothing like we had ever experienced before. Really, to be honest, have not since either, probably because it was illegal in forty-six states. Topless waitresses were bringing you free drinks as long as you were gambling. Us, coming from a small town we had never even remotely seen anything like this place before. I did not drink or gamble but this place was freaking awesome!

I sat at the blackjack table and watched Terry play 21, he kept losing his money and going to the ATM to get more. After about an hour he said, "This is the last time I am going to the ATM machine." I said, "Good, I am ready to go home." When he came back from the ATM he had a bad look on his face. He said, "You got any money?" I laughed and said, "You ain't gambling with my money!"

He said, "No. The ATM says that I have overdrawn my account and it will not give me any more money!" I said, "Well, how much money do you have on you? Let's get the hell out of here." He said, "I do not have anything left. I spent it all on blackjack." He said, "How much do you have? We need gas to get home." I pulled my money out and counted it, I had $28 to my name.

You see Terry was supposed to buy the gas on this trip and pay for the room. Because he was going to the convention whether I went or not. All I was supposed to buy was my food, as usual, we were screwed! We are eight hundred miles from home and we can not get there with $28! We sat down to think about it, while he finished his free drink. He said, "Here is what we do. Give me the $28 and I will play blackjack again and win some money, and we will go home." I said, "B. S. You already lost $200 man." He said, "Come on, I can win! I know I can! and if I don't, we have to call mom."

So, I gave him the $28, he put it all down on the first hand. He got twenty-one and won about $112, and we got the hell out of there! I drove the rest of the way home and slept for two days straight... There are so many life lessons here y'all that I do not even know where to start... You figure it out.

We had a ball on that trip though, and I wouldn't trade those teenage years' memories for the world. You talk about a road trip, two guys, and a truck. What else do you need...

Chapter Sixteen
It's Just a Piece of Metal

Ouch!

I worked on the hay wagon for six summers in a row, when I was a teenager. I always used a hay hook in my right hand but most guys do it without a hook. They just grab both wires, one in each hand, and pick the bale up. I would stab my hook at the end of the bale and then grab a wire with my left hand and pick it up that way. I felt like this gave me more leverage and control over the bale. So, I always used a hook and I always had my hook with me.

Randy's hay wagon was a Dew-Eze Hay Monster. It was basically just made out of an old school bus. They had taken the top off of the bus and all the seats out, just leaving a forty- foot long flatbed trailer. There was only the driver's seat and steering wheel. The engine and transmission were mounted underneath the bus, between the frame rails.

There was a long conveyor chain that went all the way down the middle of the bed. There was a twelve-foot snout on the front of the wagon that worked on giant hydraulic sleeves, so you could raise the snout up and down. The snout had its own conveyor chain with big spikes on it to grab ahold of the hay bales as you drove around in the field and take them to the back of the bus.

You needed three men to run this operation. One guy driving and two guys in the back, one on each side, staking the bales as they came up the conveyor chain. In a pinch, you could do this with two guys, as we did about half the time, one guy driving and one guy stacking. Who do you think was driving? Probably the guy that owned the wagon, right?

This left me to stack by myself a lot because good help is hard to find and even harder to keep. We put up a lot of hay those years and I enjoyed the work being outside and all. It was hard work but very rewarding. The people we worked for, the farmers around town, were the salt of the earth and you could not find better people.

Anyway, when you got the wagon full you had to go unload it and stack the hay in the barn. This was the hardest part of the job because if it was a hundred degrees outside, it was 130 or 140 degrees inside the barn. I know this because just out of curiosity we carried an old thermometer around with us. Plus, there was no way to get any breeze inside the barn.

One of the problems we had was the design of the snout. It worked great out in the field picking up bales, but in the barn, with it only twelve feet long it will not reach the top of the barn. However, the farmer wants the hay stacked all the way to the top of his barn. So he can get as much as possible inside and keep it out of the weather. Most barns are way more than twelve feet tall. Some are twenty-five or thirty feet tall, lofts can be even higher.

To get the hay that high you would stack up twelve or fourteen feet high. Then you had to walk around on the top layer with the snout as high as it would go. You would get down on your knees and reach way down and stab the next bale with your hook. Then pull it up to you and carry it over and stack it.

The higher your stack got the farther you had to reach down for the next bale, and the higher you got the more dangerous it became. Because at some point you were hanging down in such a peculiar manner that you could not really balance and support yourself. So, more than once I fell off the stack, and more than once, I stabbed myself with the hay hook trying to snag the next bale of hay.

One time I reached and stabbed a bale of hay and totally missed. I stabbed myself in the left thigh with the hook, and it went so deep that when I turned loose of the hook it supported itself in midair. I looked down just in awe that it could have gone in deep enough to support itself. I stood there a second looking at it, reached down, and pulled it out. Well, I did not really pull it out, it is like a giant fish hook. To get it out I had to push down and away from my thigh. It did not appear to be bleeding much, so I went back to work.

Barns are dark though and it is hard to see. I stacked the next bale and when I came back to the doorway where the sunlight came through. I could see my whole left pants leg was just saturated with blood. I jumped off the stack, ran to the water hose, pulled my pants down, and washed it off to take a look. It was not too bad and I asked the farmer, who we were working for, for some bandages. I wrapped it up and went back to work.

Another time was when I was way up in the top of a barn and reached down as far as I could to stab the next bale and missed. It was too far and I was holding the side of the snout with my left hand trying to support my entire weight with my left hand. I reached as far as I could and swung the hay hook with all the strength in my right arm. Hoping to stab it deep enough into the next bale. Then, the hook would have helped support my body weight. but I missed it. Instead of stabbing into the bale, I guess because of the weird angle, my hook just glanced off the side of the bale and went directly into my left forearm. At that point, I lost my balance and fell about fifteen feet to the ground.

A hay hook is kind of like a pencil, as you use the hook for weeks and months, stabbing it into hay bales, it gets sharper and sharper, the point gets more defined and thinner. About twice a year I would break the tip off of my hay hook and have to buy a new one. Like when you first sharpen a pencil and you press down on your paper and break the tip off.

Somehow that day when I stabbed myself in the left forearm and fell off of the stack. I broke the end of my hook off in my left forearm about an inch and a half deep, I guess because of the angle or the way I landed on it, my weight had broken the tip completely off in my arm. I stood up and looked at my arm, just before I fell, I felt and saw the hook hit my arm. Now it was bleeding and you could see a big swollen or welt looking spot in the middle of my forearm. I picked up the hook and could see it was broken off. Putting two and two together, I quickly realized there was a big hunk of metal in my arm.

What do you do now? I can not just pull it out and go back to work, it is broken off inside me! They wrapped it up and took me to the hospital. The doctor x-rayed it and said, "Yep, there is a piece of metal in your arm! It is about the size of a nickel". I am thinking, "Yeah, I know doc." He said, "We can either operate and get it out or just leave it in there. It is in the muscle and not against anything vital, we can probably just leave it there. Guys come home from war all the time with shrapnel and live their whole lives without taking it out." I was thinking, I do not have any health insurance and surgery sounds expensive. Plus, I was not sure I wanted that (one horse) town doctor cutting into me anyway.

So, the piece of metal is still with me. It has been in my arm since I was seventeen. It sets off metal detectors at airports and places, but it is a hell of a conversation piece.

All three of my kids when they were little and sat on my lap would rub my arm and ask me, "Daddy, how did you get that piece of metal in your arm?" You can see it and feel it sticking up in the middle of my left forearm. I always had a story to tell them, and I have told it a thousand different ways.

I would say, "Well, I was in the jungles of Laos, in Vietnam, and my weapon jammed." Or I would say, "I was in Desert Storm and stepped on a landmine!" and their eyes would get bigger and bigger. Or I would say, "I used to be a pilot and my plane went down over the Nile River one time." Or I would say, "I used to drive NASCAR, and the King put me in the wall in '76", and their eyes would get bigger and bigger.

You see where I am going with this right? They always loved to ask me how I got that piece of metal in my arm and I always had a story to tell them. It worked great for bedtime stories.

If you asked any of my three kids today, how I got this piece of metal in my arm, you would get ten different stories. In fact, if you asked it with them all in the same room, you would probably get thirty different stories as they argued back and forth about it. "No! It wasn't like that! It was like this!" And "No! He didn't do that! He did this!" We still laugh about it every time it comes up... It's just a piece of metal.

Chapter Seventeen

Hodgepodge

Stupid Is Stupid Does

Did you ever do anything really stupid? I did! One winter just to make some extra money on the side, Terry and I cut and sold firewood. We were probably about sixteen or seventeen. We would go out in the country somewhere, it may have been the property of somebody we knew or it may not have been. I am not at liberty to say. Plus if I told you, I would have to kill you:).

Anyway, we would cut a bunch of wood and throw it in the back of Terry's pickup. Then we would take it to his mom's house and split it and stack it in her backyard. Then people would come by and we would load it in their truck and sell it to them for $50 a rick. We had to split the wood by hand because we could not afford an automatic wood splitter.

Have you tried splitting a piece of wood with an ax and every time you hit it, it jumps about a foot and you keep hitting it and chasing it all over the yard? Well, it happened to me. I hit this piece of wood and it flew about two feet, and I had to move over and hit it again. It kept moving and I kept chasing it and hitting it again. Then, after about five or six times I was really getting mad.

I swung the ax back as hard as I could and was about to knock the crap out of that piece of wood. When all of a sudden, my ax got caught up with Terry's mom's clothesline wire that went down one side of her backyard. It acted like a spring-loaded device. Just as I looked up, the ax came flying back and hit me right in the forehead, right between my eyes!

Well, you know how a wound on the face is, it just started gushing blood, I was bleeding like a stuck pig. It was running down my face and into my eyes and I could not see anything. I ran into the house. Terry's mom was a nurse by trade, a good thing for us, right? She cleaned it up and Terry ran me to the hospital, they stitched me back up again. They pulled my file, which looked like an encyclopedia by now, and said, "Well, you are not allergic to anything. We will give you some penicillin for infection and some pain medicine", and they sent me home. They said that I was lucky because one inch to either side would have put an eye out!

Luckily for me, I had been using a (single) blade ax that day and just the butt of it hit me between the eyes. Had it been a (double) edged ax, I would not be writing this book right now. Really stupid... Lesson learned.

Kidney Stones

After I burned our house down on the west side of town baby Melissa, Christy, and I moved in with Christy's parents. It was my last resort, trust me, I did not want to live with the in-laws, but there was nowhere else to go. We had lost everything in the fire and I did not have two nickels to rub together. Christy's father always hated me though. No matter how hard I worked or how hard I tried to fix it, I am and shall always be the guy who got his teenage daughter pregnant, and for that, I will always be the enemy. That sucked too because he had been a mechanic for the City of Guthrie until he retired after twenty-five years. I had taken two years of auto mechanics at the Vo-tech in high school and a year and a half in the GM training program in college. We would have a lot in common, you would think.

The whole time I knew him, including the six months I lived in his house after the fire, he has never said three words to me. We could have been close and I could have learned a lot from him in those early years, not to be though, he hated me.

We had been staying with my in-laws for about two weeks. I came home one evening from work and the only people in the house were baby Melissa and Christy's mom. Christy's mom never drove a car, she never learned how and never had a license. I went into the back and was playing with the baby, Christy's mom was in the living room watching TV.

All of a sudden, I got this terrible sharp pain on the left side of my lower back and side. Nothing like I had ever felt before! I started sweating and felt feverish. I stood up and thought I was going to faint from the unbearable pain. I stumbled into the kitchen and tried to grab the back of a chair, but fell down. Christy's mom looked up and screamed. I did not understand what was happening, I thought I was dying.

Her mom could not drive or take me to the hospital. I had to call my mom and wait for fifteen minutes for her to get there and take me to the hospital. By the time I got to the hospital, I was screaming in pain. I remember saying, "Doc, what the hell is wrong, am I dying?" The pain was unbearable. On a pain scale from one to ten, it was twelve! They ran a bunch of tests and said that I had kidney stones. They said, "You will pass it pretty soon and the pain will be over." The doctor said that kidney stone pain is the closest a man can ever come to actual labor pain. He said, "It is a calcium deposit. If you will not eat foods high in calcium, you will probably never have another kidney stone." After that, I avoided milk, cheese, and butter, like they were the plague.

Over the next five years, I would have two more kidney stones. I passed the first two but they had to go in and get the last one. I am not even going to tell you how they go in and get one, it still hurts just to talk about it twenty-five years later. Okay, they take this long wire thing with a giant retractable claw on the end of it. Umm, never mind.

All those kidney stones happened in Guthrie, the first one when I was nineteen. The third one, which they went in and removed, they gave it to me. I still have it in a sandwich baggy. It looks like a jagged shard of something from another planet. I cannot believe it came from inside me.

Twenty years later, I woke up one morning and I could not walk. My left foot and ankle were all swollen and purple and red looking, I could not even get my boot on. I went to the doctor because I could not walk and the pain was terrible. After running a bunch of tests he said, "You have gout, and there is too much uric acid in your body. Be careful, because too much uric acid will give you a kidney stone." I said, "What the hell are you talking about?" I said, "I had a bunch of kidney stones twenty-five years ago and the doctor told me it was calcium deposits that cause kidney stones. He told me to stay away from calcium." I said, "I have not had cheese on my cheeseburger in twenty-five years. I have avoided dairy products like it was the plague".

He said, "No! There are only two things that cause kidney stones, one is the calcium deposits. The other one is uric acid crystals that build up in your joints and break loose, they travel into your bloodstream and go to your kidneys. You get uric acid from bread, pasta, beer, and things like that, not from calcium. If you have gout, you usually have kidney stones from it. Did they send your stone to the lab to see if it was calcium or uric acid?"

I said, "Hell no! They gave it to me. I still have it." He said, "Nowadays, we are required to send any kidney stone we get to the lab. This way we can tell the patient what foods to avoid, based on what it is made of." I said, "Man, I have been avoiding the wrong stuff for twenty-five years!" He said, "Yes, it sure does look like it." I had been screwed by that (one horse) town doctor again!

Like Father Like Son

Remember when I said if you are a real man you lead by example because your kids will grow up wanting to be just like their daddy? Remember when I said my dad always carried his pocket knife and taught me to do the same? Well, my dad also had his

Chapstick in his pocket, always. He would carry the same tube around for years until it was absolutely worn out, with the label worn completely off. It would be an ugly-looking, (off-white) almost brown-looking unrecognizable thing. It was all scratched up and worn from being in his pocket every day with his keys and knife.

He only used the original Chapstick flavor. He would never use the new-fangled fancy flavors, like blueberry or strawberry. It was his, and his only. If you asked to use it you always got NO!

Well, like father like son because I have always carried Chapstick in my pocket for as long as I can remember, However, I like the cherry flavor, and if I know you, I will probably share.

I have told people all my life that I have never been addicted to anything except Chapstick. I do not drink or smoke, and I have never had an illegal drug in my body.

But there is nothing like a hit of Chapstick, am I

right? Especially on a hot dry day, nothing else will do, and I admit it, I am an addict! Just talking about it makes me want to take a hit right now:).

Family Reunion

During my teenage years, I used to go with my grandma and grandpa to our family reunion. It was held each summer in west Texas, around the Fourth of July. Each year it was held in a different location in west Texas, usually around a lake or state park area.

One year when I was fifteen, we drove out there from Oklahoma City. It was my grandpa and grandma and me and one of my younger cousins. We drove in my grandparents' car to west Texas. This particular year it was held around Big Spring Texas, at Lake Thomas. We were there for three days over the Fourth of July weekend, it was a blast. I saw people I had not seen in years. People would come up to me that I did not know, and they knew exactly who I was. As I said, I looked like my dad and they would recognize me.

I had a great aunt who lived in west Texas and we were pen pals ever since I was a youngster. I always loved to see her, she was my favorite aunt, the reunion was always a lot of fun. There were fishing and cookouts and tons of activities for the kids, being right on the lake. They rented a giant cabin and there would be forty or fifty of us staying in this huge cabin for three days. We would set up cots and I remember sleeping on the back screened-in porch with my cousin.

On the evening of the fourth of July, just around dark. About twenty of us got into my uncle's bass boat and went down to the marina to watch the huge fireworks show they were having over the water. Hundreds of boats showed up for the show, it was bumper-to-bumper boats in the marina. We had a blast, just talking with people on the other boats and getting to know each other. Everybody was taking pictures of each other and the fireworks show. The fireworks show was spectacular and it lasted for about thirty minutes.

As soon as the show ended, all the boats took off at once. The wake and waves created by all those boats moving at once were huge! Our problem was that we had not thought this whole thing through very well. None of us were wearing life jackets! We had about twenty people on a small bass boat, which was only supposed to carry around five or six people on a normal day.

My uncle, who was driving the boat, did his best to steer, I am sure. However, with all those giant waves the boat I was on was doomed! Our boat flipped over in the middle of the lake. It was so dark that you could not see anything.

We all went into the water without life jackets on. People were just screaming and flopping around everywhere. Other boats were still flying by, and they could not see all the people in the water in the pitch-dark conditions. Most of us swam to shore, which was probably two hundred yards. I had an older cousin who had swum in college and almost made the Olympic team. Thank God that he was there, he spent a good thirty minutes helping people get out of the water.

When we all got back to shore, they did a headcount, there were still three or four people missing. It turned out that the ones missing had been picked up by some other boats out on the lake. After about an hour of chaos, everyone was accounted for. Man, we were lucky that night that no one drowned. The next morning as we left, that bass boat was still upside down by the bank, where it had washed up. As I said, it is a wonder we survived those teenage years!

Another valuable life lesson learned at an early age for me though. Every time my kids get on my boat. Everyone must have their life jacket on before we leave the dock because you never know. It is always better to be prepared, I even carry extra life jackets, just in case. You should too.

Don't Shoplift!

When I was fourteen, shortly after I came to Guthrie, I had been hearing the kids at school talking about shoplifting around town and getting away with it. I remember one kid saying that he stole some pencils or something and another said that he got away with a pair of shoes.

One day, mom and I were in the grocery store. I had always followed directly behind her at the store in a single line. The first time she saw me do this she thought it was very strange and asked me why I followed in a straight line and did not speak in the store. I said, "Because that is the way Brenda had taught me and my sister to walk in a store, and if we did not stay quiet and follow in a straight line, we would get a beating when we got home!" So, this time at the grocery store mom told me to go ahead and look around while she did her shopping.

I was walking through the aisles when I remembered what those kids had said the day before at school. I wondered if I could get away with taking a pack of gum or something. I was nervous, but I very nonchalantly picked up a pack of gum and acted like I was reading the ingredients or something. Then, very carefully I slid it into my pocket. That was not so bad, I thought, and after a few minutes, I did it again. Then, I put a couple of Slim Jim's in my pocket. Wow, that was easy, I thought. Then, for the next fifteen minutes or so, I kept sticking things in my pockets. First the front pockets and then the back.

All of a sudden, some guy grabbed my arm. He said, "I saw you put something in your pocket!" He led me straight to the manager's office. The manager said, "This is an undercover agent we have here at the store, and he says you put something in your pocket." He said, "Did you put something in your pocket?" I said, "No!" He said, "I can see something bulging in your pocket. Why don't you take it out and lay it on my desk?"

I said, "That's just my keys or knife or something." He said, "Take it out or I will have to call the police." I quickly pulled a Slim Jim out and laid it on his desk. He said, "Where are your parents?" I said, "My mom is shopping here in the store." I told him her name. He left the office and went and hollered at her on the loudspeaker.

While he was gone, I emptied my pockets. I had twenty or twenty-five items in my front and rear pockets and even some things stuck in my socks. I had candy, gum, beef jerky, you name it. I threw it all behind a large filing cabinet in his office. A few minutes later, he came back in with mom. I was so scared and embarrassed and mortified.

He told mom that since it was just a .29 cent, Slim Jim, he was not going to press charges. But she needed to get me out of his store and keep me out! He said that if I ever did that again he would just call the police instead of going and finding my mom. I explained to mom that the kids at school had been talking about it, and I just wanted to see if it was as easy as they made it sound. Man, was she mad and embarrassed, Lesson Learned! I have never shoplifted anything since. Can you imagine the look on the cleaning lady's face when she cleaned behind that filing cabinet? ha-ha

Terry's first job when he was sixteen, was being a bag boy at that very grocery store. I often wanted to stop in and say, "Hi," while he was working. But I was too scared to go back to that store and face that manager. When mom would go there and grocery shop, I would sit in the car. I never went back in until several years later when it changed from IGA to Homeland grocery and got a new manager.

They did not have cameras in stores in the '80s as they do nowadays. I did not know it but apparently, they had plainclothes security guys walking around keeping an eye on things. As I said, I learned everything the hard way.

I know it is hard on you guys as teenagers today. With peer pressure or just friends telling you they got away with shoplifting, trust me it is not worth it. You do not want to go to jail over a pair of shoes or a new T-shirt. So my advice here is just do not do it. Don't allow yourself to bow down to peer pressure. Plus, the embarrassment of getting caught is almost unbearable. Once you get caught you will be labeled a thief from now on. It is just not worth it guys, trust me. Don't shoplift!!!

Jazzercise

My junior year in high school was the first year Guthrie High School had ever offered a weight-lifting class as an elective. Before that, I could only get into the weight room if the football team or wrestling team were down there working out and the door was unlocked. The coaches knew me and would let me work out with the team even though I was not on the team. But we never had a real weight-lifting class offered before.

I was one of the first students to sign up when they offered the class. However, the weight-lifting class was only one semester. The other half of the year was the Jazzercise class. In 1986, I had never seen a Jazzercise class before and was not exactly sure what it was about. But I wanted to be in the weight-lifting class really bad and signed up. The Jazzercise class was in the first semester and the weight-lifting class was in the second semester. The first day of school that year was an eye-opening experience for me to say the least. The Jazzercise class had twenty-six girls, me, and a guy named Keith who I knew from shop class.

Keith and I just stood in the back of the class in awe as we watched all those girls in their tight little workout suits jumping around for forty-five minutes each day. The instructor lady got on to us every day for just standing there doing nothing all class long. That is the only workout class I ever took where I did not even break a sweat. Keith and I just stood in the back and watched all those girls bending and jumping every day for that first semester. What a class! When the other students found out we were the only two boys in the whole class, they just laughed and laughed.

We explained to the rest of the student body that this was the best class ever invented. All we did was stand in the back and watch the girls jump around in their tight outfits., and the instructor wasn't bad to look at either.

I was not in that weight-lifting/Jazzercise class the following year. During my senior year, I only needed three credits to graduate. I left school every day at about 11:30 a.m. and went to work. So I did not take any electives in my senior year. But I bet half that class was boys after Keith and I explained it to everybody.

The second semester was weight lifting. Keith was on the yearbook staff and always had his camera with him. One day he talked me into posing in the weight room, working out with weights, for yearbook pictures. He took five or six pictures of me working out on different machines. A couple of months later when the yearbook came out, I was all excited to get my yearbook and check out my pictures.

There was a whole page in the yearbook dedicated to talking about this new and exciting weight-lifting/Jazzercise class they were now offering at our high school. There were three or four big pictures of me working out. You could tell it was me because I had on my classic blue shorts and a sleeveless T-shirt that I always wore in the weight room.

Keith and I knew that I had posed for all those pictures, but they put some other kid's name under all my pictures! You could not see my face in any of the shots. Keith had tried to get the weights in the shots and was not concentrating on getting my face. For instance, he had me on the bench press, pressing 300 pounds, but he took the picture on his knees, from below my feet. The picture showed up my body and across my chest, and all the weight I was lifting, but you could not see my face because of the angle of the camera.

On the lat machine, he had taken a picture of my back to show the detail in my arms and back as I pulled the weight down. On the leg press, all you could see were my knees and legs and the weights I was lifting. You could not see my face in any of the shots.

In the 1980s the camera did not show you the picture you were taking instantly. Like cell phones or digital cameras do today. In the '80s you had to manually develop the film before you could ever see the pictures you took. So it might be days before you know if you made a mistake or not. Keith had not gotten my face in any of the pictures he took that day in the weight room. When I got my yearbook, I ran and found Keith and asked him what had happened. He said that on the day they edited those pictures he was absent, and someone else had put the wrong name under the pictures because they could not see my face.

He said that by the time they noticed the mistake, it was too late and the yearbooks were already in print. I kept that yearbook for about ten years, then, I finally threw it away. I could not stand looking at my pictures with someone else's name under them.

Wrong High School

One day in high school, Terry and I and two of our friends all skipped school for the day. We planned to go to Oklahoma City and go into another high school and check out the talent! That is the girls to you guys:). We drove to Oklahoma City and stopped for lunch at a Domino's Pizza place, we had never eaten at a Domino's before. Growing up in a small town, we only had a McDonald's and a Sonic for fast food. The only pizza place in town was Pizza Hut.

Terry and I went in and got a large pizza with everything on it. We took it back to the car, we four guys devoured it in about three minutes. We went right back in and got another one just like it. After lunch, we drove around until we found a high school. We did not really know where we were going, we had never been there before. When we got to the high school parking lot, the other two kids chickened out and would not go inside. So Terry and I went in without them.

We were walking down the hall just looking around when this lady came up to us and asked for our hall pass. We said that we did not have one. She said, "Well go to the office and get one then." So we went to the office and asked for hall passes. The lady in the office said, "What is your name?" I said, "Joe Smith." I do not remember what Terry said. We got our hall passes and wandered around for about twenty minutes, just checking out girls and looking around the school.

We went back to the car and the other guys said, "You sure were in there for a long time. We thought you got arrested or something." We showed them our hall passes, and we laughed and laughed all the way back to Guthrie.

In my entire adult life, every time I did not want to give my real name, I tell people my name is Joe Smith. For the past fifteen years, I have been buying and selling cars. I have a tow truck and I take a lot of old cars to the crusher down on the south side of town. The first time I went in there I was not sure I wanted my name on the ticket, so I told them my name was Joe Smith.

So, for fifteen years they have been putting Joe Smith on my tickets, even though my name is right on the front of my work shirts. There are four or five guys that work there and they all know me because I have been coming in for so long. Every time I go in, they always say, "Hey, Joe, What's up?" Even though my name is right on the front of my shirt. How funny is that?

Just F. Y. I.

When I worked at the furniture store in high

school, I asked Mike one day. "What is the thing here that you make the most money on when you sell it?" He said, "By far, it is the refrigerators. The markup on most of the furniture here is about 100 percent. But the markup on refrigerators is closer to 300 percent." I asked, "Why?" He said, "Because they are made in China with cheap labor and cheap parts." I said, "Well, why don't you just sell them cheap?" He said, "Because a refrigerator is something people only buy once or twice in their whole life. And they expect to pay a lot for something that lasts that long."

When I was in college in the G. M. Training program, we spent one day touring the G. M. Assembly plant here in Oklahoma City. At the end of the tour, I asked the guide, "How much money do you have in a car when it rolls off the assembly line?" He said, "About $3,500." Then, we sell it to the dealership for around "$7,000." At the time, I was working at a local Buick dealership where they sold those very A-Body G. M. cars that they made right here in town at the G. M.

Assembly plant. I know for a fact that they sold them every day where I worked for $14,900. Are you learning anything here yet?

What I am saying is that virtually everything you buy has at least a 100 percent markup on it, at a retail store, not only automobiles and houses. Every time you buy something, from furniture and bedding to TVs and electronics and refrigerators. If you are paying cash, you can always haggle them down because the markup is so high. Just like when you buy a car and try to get a better price. This even works at the grocery store, if you can find a small-town grocery because you need to be speaking to the owner, not the manager. But it does not work as well at large chain grocery stores. I am serious, try it for yourself sometime and see. How much money could you save over your lifetime? If you could get 10 percent or 15 percent or more off of everything you bought?

Bill

Shortly after I moved to my mom's house in 1981, I met her father for the first time. My Grandfather was born in 1900, so, when I met him, he was 81 years old. His name was Harry but his friends called him Bill. He was 4ft. 11 inches tall. He had only had one job in his entire life. he spent 33 years in the U.S Army. In 1917, he joined the Army at the age of 17. He told me that he changed the date on his birth certificate and lied and told them that he was 18 years old.

So, 100 years ago this year he went to France to fight for freedom in WWI. Then in 1942, he fought in WWII after the Japanese bombed Pearl Harbor. He once told me he had been to Germany, France, Italy, Japan, the Philippians, Austria, and many other places during his 33 years in the Army. The stories he would tell about his adventures.

He retired in 1950 from the Army, I wish I had known him in his earlier years, his stories were fascinating. He was a second-degree black belt and had spent half of his life learning hand-to-hand combat. I was told by several people that he could kick a six-foot man in the head, even into his seventies. I only knew him during my teenage years because he passed away in 1990. I believe it is up to the children and grandchildren of the guys who were there, to keep telling their stories and keep their legacy alive.

I wish I had taken notes of the stories he told me during the 1980s and my teenage years. His life would have made a much more fascinating book than my life. I often thought that if I could just be half the man Bill was, I could change the world. I wonder how many of us would have the patriotism, or the guts to lie about our age and join a world war at the age of 17, that was a real man!

When I was 17 he gave me a box filled with metals and old coins from his time in the military. Inside the box was an old beat-up and scarred pair of brass knuckles. He told me that he had carried them in his pocket all throughout WWI and WWII. Every time I pick up that old pair of brass knuckles, I think about Bill. I wish those knuckles could talk, the stories they could tell. The places they have been and the things they have seen. I am going to give them to my son someday and tell him all the stories of my grandfather.

Thanks, Bill, for all your service and hard work, and thanks to all the veterans who have sacrificed so much and given so much for our freedom that most of us take for granted. Freedom is not free, you have to fight for it! Just ask Bill.

God bless America and all of our fighting men and women overseas and around the world. Please, bring them home safely.

Chapter Eighteen

Terry and My Dad

Terry and my dad never met, but I believe they would have liked each other because they were a lot alike. They both weighed about 350 lbs. Dad smoked like a freight train, and that is what killed him. Terry drank like a fish, and that is what killed him.

I have only been to one funeral in my whole life. (I do not do funerals.) It was in July 2016 when I went to Terry's funeral, my dad died six years earlier, in 2010. Katie and I drove to Wisconsin to see him two days before he died but did not stay for the funeral. This was a man I had never seen show emotion, I had never seen him cry. He had never told me he loved me, he had never even patted me on the back and said 'I'm proud of you son.'

My sister and I walked into his room at the

hospital, where he was lying on his deathbed. We were standing on either side of his bed. He reached up and grabbed us, one in each arm around our necks, and pulled us down to his face. He says, in a real stern voice, "I love you guys, and I mean it!" We both just burst into tears, bawling our eyes out.

We walked out in the hall and Katie said, "T. J., I have craved that my entire life! I have just craved that man to show me some affection and love. Why did he have to wait until he was dead to say something!?" She said, "It is too late! It's too late! It's just too late."

So, I challenge you guys again! When you go home today hug your kids, your grandkids, or your spouse and tell them that you love them. Tell them you are proud of them. Tell them you are glad you got to be a part of their lives. Life goes by so quickly y'all, it could all be over tomorrow, and It is too late. If you do this it will not make you any less of a man. In fact, in my eyes, it will make you a better man, and they are probably craving it! They are probably craving it.

I went to see Terry two weeks before he died. We talked about everything, from his mom to the werewolf to the Brown Beast. I told him that I was going to write a book someday about our teenage years. (He said if I did that I needed to put his name on it:). My name is James Wray, the T. in T.J. Wray is for Terry). We talked for two hours about everything, but what stuck out to me the most was when he talked for probably twenty minutes about his two daughters and how proud he was of them.

He said that the oldest one had just enrolled at the same college Terry went to and was in the x-ray field just as he had been some twenty-five years earlier. Then, he went on and on about the youngest one and how she had the singing voice of an angel. He told me how she sang in the church choir and how she had even traveled overseas with the church to sing in the choir. He thought that she would probably grow up to be a great musician. Man, he was sure proud of those girls, as all fathers should be in my eyes.

My dad always said that his legacy was a gun collection that he had been collecting all of his life. When he died, he had over seventy guns, but he could not take them with him, so what good are they to him now?

I am here to tell you guys that your legacy is your children and grandchildren and the way you treated people in the short time you had here on earth. Not a bunch of junk you collected over your life. My dad was a smart man in many ways, but he got this one wrong! You need to take care of your kids and grandkids, that is your legacy, I could never get my dad to understand this. So long, Dad, I miss you. So long Terry, I miss you too buddy.

I only have two regrets in my life, most of the things that happened in my life I would not change if I could. Even the bad stuff because it was a good life lesson that helped me later in becoming the man I am today.

However, like I said I was a year older than Terry. So when I turned twenty-one, he used to come and get me and buy me a hamburger or something. Then I would go inside the liquor store and get him a bottle. We did this a lot during that year until he turned twenty-one. I have always regretted doing that, and I would like to apologize to his family and his mom. She would have kicked my ass if she had known I was doing that, and I am sorry.

No one else but Terry and I ever knew I had done this, and I wish I could go back and change it. Now that he is gone, I feel like I contributed to his being an alcoholic, because I bought the alcohol that year, and I am sorry. He probably would have found another way to get it, but I still should not have done it.

The only other regret is when Terry's mother died, she had me on the list to be a pallbearer. I did not go because I do not do funerals, I have always regretted that. She was always there for me in my teenage years, and I should have been there for her in the end, and for that, I am also sorry.

Now that I look back. I wish I had gone to Terry's mom's funeral and my dad's funeral, hindsight though, right?

Chapter Nineteen

The End

My kids always tell me that I am old. Any subject that comes up seems to take me back to the '80s and my teenage years. In 1981, I was thirteen and in 1988, I was nineteen. It does not matter what subject you are talking about. If it is religion, it takes me back to Ms. Norma's Sunday school class and all the things we talked about, and all the Bible classes we studied as teenagers. Or if it is camping, fishing, cooking out, shooting guns, building campfires, pitching a tent, and all the other things I did for the first time in my teenage years in Royal Rangers, which is the church's version of Boy Scouts.

Or my first game of pool, which I shot when I was fourteen against the pastor of our church. I was in the game room of the bowling alley, where I had gone with our youth group when Pastor walked by on his way to the bathroom, I think. He asked me if I wanted to shoot a game. I said, "I don't know how," and he said, "Come on, I will show you."

He taught me how to break and a little about banks and English. I love to shoot pool and remember that first game often. He is the same guy who married Christy and me when I was eighteen. He taught me a lot of good life lessons. On my wedding day, I still remember him saying for me to live my life as an example to my children. I still try to live like that today...

Or music. To this day my favorite CD is "Back in Black" by AC/DC, it came out in 1980. I bought the cassette tape in the early 1980s with one of those Publishers Clearing House, (get thirteen tapes for a penny deals). I know y'all did the same thing I did. You ordered the thirteen for a penny and instead of buying ten more at regular prices, you canceled your subscription and never bought anything else. Right?

I bought 'Back in Black,' and when it came, my mom took it away from me. Saying it was Devil's music and I was not allowed to have it. Later when I moved out at eighteen, I took the cassette tape from her dresser drawer and I wore it out. To this day it is one of my favorite albums, I like every song on it. There is a CD of it in my truck right now. If you do not own it, go get it, you will love it.

Who would have ever dreamed Oklahoma City would get a professional basketball team, name them the (Thunder), and they would come running out onto the court every night to an AC/DC song? Devil's music according to my mother.

When Terry and I were in Amway we had a saying, (S.I.B.K.I.S.). This meant, (see it big, keep it simple). Probably my favorite song of all time is (Simple Man), by Lynyrd Skynyrd. I tell my son all the time. That when I am dead and gone if he needs any fatherly advice. Just refer to this song and keep it simple, be a simple man. If you guys want to hear something awesome, listen to Shinedowns remake of ' Simple Man'.

Or movies. The first Back to the Future movie came out in 1985 and is still one of my favorites, or Rocky or Rambo, or the value of a dollar or the value of a hard day's work. All these things I learned in my early teenage years have stuck with me my entire lifetime.

I worked on the Hay Wagon for Randy, for six summers. The first day on the Hay Wagon when I was thirteen, I will never forget. I weighed about 130 pounds and the green alfalfa hay bales we were hauling weighed more than I did. We were stacking them in the loft of an old barn, it was June and about 100 degrees outside. It was probably 140 degrees in that loft of that barn and I thought I was going to die of heatstroke.

Randy and I topped out that loft, he carried the bales, but I was too small and weak. I had to drag the bale over to the stack and with all my might, I had to pick it up and push it up on top of the next bale. I was moving one bale to Randy's three. He later told me that after that first day he thought he would never see me again. Somehow though, sunburnt to a crisp and hands blistered to the bone, I came back the next day for more and stayed for six years. I get emotional just writing this stuff guys, but I learned so many great life lessons on those first few jobs that helped me in many ways throughout my life. What I refer to as sweat equity, or old school, small-town values. Which are getting harder and harder to find these days.

I used to judge the value of things by how many bales of hay I had to haul to be able to buy it. For instance, if I wanted a new cassette tape or tool or even a new truck or motorcycle, I would do the math. I got paid ten cents a bale. This meant that I had to pick a bale of hay up in the field, put it on the hay wagon, take it to the barn and unload and stack it to get ten cents. So, if a cassette tape cost $8, I had to haul eighty bales of hay to get it.

If you think like this you will spend your money

very wisely, especially when it is 140 degrees in those barns. Like I said these lessons and values have stuck with me my entire life, and I am glad I went through them to make me the man I am today. I am forty-eight and I have never owned a credit card. I am debt-free and my house is paid for, I am a single father with two teenagers, no one has ever helped me or given me anything. I learned at an early age if you want something just put in the work and go earn it. I have always just saved up and paid cash for whatever I wanted. Maybe if everybody in America thought like this our country would not be buried in debt and paying twenty percent interest on it:).

To everyone who reads this. God bless you and your family and thank you very much... T.J. and Terry

----

I would like to suggest that the next book you read is (Dig Deep) by J.C. Watts. This book will change your life. It will teach you to dig deep and find inside yourself a better version of you, that God always intended for you to be. It will teach you to set goals and take responsibility for your life. Read it! I dare you...

Me in 1981… I know, What a goober right?

1982

My Royal Ranger uniform. Everyone said I looked all grown up.

1983

My truck the day I brought it home. I wish I had a picture to show you when I got it finished. It was candy apple red with white wagon wheels. It was beautiful and I loved that truck.

1986

Margaret and I, at the prom.

1987

Terry and I at high school graduation. I know it is hard to see, but we are the two in the middle with shades on:).

1987

You should have seen that teacher's face when he saw my sunglasses. Priceless:)

1988

My Dad and I, with baby Melissa.

This is a picture of a Hay Monster hay wagon I found on the Internet. They only made these in the 1970s and '80s. By the 1990s most farmers had gone to the giant round hay bales you still see everywhere today. Making these square bale hauling machines obsolete.

In ancient times people talked about The All-Seeing Eye or The Eye of God. This so-called (Eye of Providence) is supposed to be able to see the entire universe at one time. It is said that it watches over all of humanity. I think it is supposed to keep you on the right path or the straight and narrow and make sure you are doing the things in your life that you were intended to do. While keeping you on the right path it helps keep you out of trouble and focused on the future.

If you will look, in America we put this symbol on our money. I believe it is on the back of the one-dollar bill. I am not sure I ever really believed in an All-Seeing

Eye. I think it is just my conscience that keeps me out of trouble and on the right path. But I do believe in God and I do think we will all be held accountable for our actions one day. I think we all have a purpose in life and should spend our time in search of that purpose. If you read (The Alchemist), the author Paulo Coelho talks about your (Personal Legend). Which I believe is your (Purpose) in life.

So, I want to challenge you guys for the third time in this book. Spend your time wisely and search for your Personal Legend, find your Purpose in life. I know as humans we all get lazy and we all procrastinate. But we need to stay focused and stay on the right path to fulfilling our purpose in life.

My sister, who is in her fifties now, never had any children, she never went to college or had a career. She spent her entire life just sitting at home while her husband went to work. All those boring days with nothing to do, floundering through life not really accomplishing anything. I often tell her she should adopt a child or take a foreign exchange student in.

Imagine all the knowledge and wisdom she could teach a child after having lived for fifty years. I believe it is our duty to pass on our father's and grandfather's knowledge to our children. I am not just singling out my sister, I have my downfalls and shortcomings too. We all get lazy and lose sight of our purpose from time to time. I am just saying find your purpose in life, your Personal Legend, and follow your dreams, and don't worry, God will keep his eye on you...

T.J.

Dedication

I would like to dedicate this book to my best friend Terry, his wife Patty, and their two daughters Kayla and Amber. Terry passed away in July 2016 at the age of forty-six. I told him I was going to write a book someday about our teenage years. If this book makes any money, I am going to give some of the profit to his wife and daughters.

At Terry's funeral, his wife asked me to get up and talk, I told two or three of the stories in this book. After the funeral, several people came up to me and said I should write a book about our wild adventures. My children had already been telling me for years that I should write a book; because they have been listening to these stories their entire lives. We all know someone who has passed away. Wouldn't it be great if we could write a book about them? To remember them by, Plus, future generations could also read about them. How cool would that be?

I would also like to dedicate this book to my dad who passed away in 2010 at the age of sixty-five. He was my inspiration growing up, and like most kids, I thought that he was superman and bulletproof. He was a hardworking old-school guy, working two jobs most of the time and just doing the best he could to raise me and my sister. I still miss him.

And last but certainly not least, to my three children and two grandchildren who are my inspiration today and every day. I love you guys.

In 1991, I was 23 years old and working at a Buick dealership in Oklahoma City. One day they fired an old man that worked there, and I broke my back in three places and pinched a nerve going to my left leg, loading his toolbox into the back of his truck. After the surgery and a week in the hospital, I spent a year and a half in rehab and physical therapy learning how to walk again. But that was the '90s, and the '90s is a whole other book...

About the Author

T. J. Wray grew up in a small town. He grew up quickly and got his first job at only thirteen years old. He knew people depended on him to do his job every day. So, for two years he never missed a day. No matter the weather conditions, he always got the job done. He learned responsibility for his actions at an early age.

He was very active in his church and with his youth group. He learned a lot from the positive role models in his church, like his youth pastor and his Sunday school teacher. He did not party or drink in high school. He was responsible and went to work after school. He got his driver's license at age fourteen and drove himself everywhere, while the other kids still rode the bus. Even though he was a teenager, he was an adult.

He really enjoyed (life in a small-town), everybody knew him and knew his truck. They would wave at him as he drove down the street. They would say hello as they passed on the sidewalk or in stores. He said that in a small-town people "actually shook hands"

In his teenage years, he was an avid fisherman. He used to travel around the state of Oklahoma looking for the best fishing holes. He once said that he would rather "fish than breathe". There is nothing that compares to hooking into a largemouth bass. He was quoted as saying, "If they don't ride motorcycles and go fishing in heaven, I don't want to go".

Nowadays he lives in the Big City. He says that nobody knows anybody, and they don't want to. He says that everyone is always in a Big Hurry, and would rather run over you than wait for one minute for you to move. No one ever seems to slow down and enjoy life in the Big City. He really misses life in a (small-town)...

If you enjoyed reading my story. Please leave a quick review on Amazon or Goodreads. Your reviews help other readers find good books they may like. It also lets the author know if they are writing something that people are enjoying. I always love to read the reviews and feedback from my readers. So please take a moment and leave a quick review. Thank you so much and Happy Reading.

This is the first book in the (My Life) series. The second book is called (The '90s - Life on the Road). Please look for my other books on Amazon and Goodreads. My latest and 3rd book is titled (The Adventures of CDL Mikey).

https://www.amazon.com/dp/B07L2CNBFV

Follow me here to get news on my giveaways and new book releases. Or to ask me about any other questions you may have.

Twitter: @TJamesWray

https://twitter.com/TJamesWray

My Website:

https://sites.google.com/view/tjwray/home

My Goodreads Author Page:

https://www.goodreads.com/author/show/17726900.T_J_Wray

Old Barns

Do you guys like old barns? Their pictures are all over my house. I guess it is from my teenage years and hauling hay for a living. I am going to drive around someday and make a scrapbook of old barns. What is it about old barns? I would rather look at an old barn than a new house.

The End

www.ingramcontent.com/pod-product-compliance
Lightning Source LLC
Chambersburg PA
CBHW071355290426
44108CB00014B/1555